TYLER FLORENCE FRESH

PHOTOGRAPHS BY JOHN LEE

CLARKSON POTTER/PUBLISHERS
NEW YORK

Copyright © 2012
by Tyler Florence
Photographs copyright © 2012
by John Lee

Library of Congress Cataloging-in-Publication
Florence, Tyler.
    Tyler Florence fresh / Tyler Florence.
        pages cm.
1. Seasonal cooking.   I. Title.
    TX714.F6364 2012
    641.5'64—dc23   2012028181

ISBN 978-0-385-34453-1
eISBN 978-0-385-34454-8

Printed in the United States of America

Design by Jan Derevjanik
Jacket photographs © 2012 by John Lee

10 9 8 7 6 5 4 3 2 1

First Edition

To my beautiful wife, Tolan,
and our three amazing children,
Miles, Hayden, and Dorothy.
You are the loves of my life.

CONTENTS

A FRESH START

I love writing about food as much as I love cooking. It's my mission, as well as my passion, to push myself and my team to discover the truth of flavor, a naked honesty that reveals itself once you start to understand the soul of the ingredients in front of you. The image your mind produces when you taste something amazing — say, a fully ripened heirloom tomato in the third week of August or the funky earthiness of white truffle in November — sends a crystal clear signal from your palate to your brain, a high-def sensation that fully completes the flavor experience. That is always the highest goal of cooking. I'm consistently fine-tuning my cooking techniques so that the signal of pure flavor and the integrity of fresh ingredients shine through. I love turning the subtle nuances of great flavor into moments that truly affect you. My goal is to give you tastes you'll never forget.

Cooking is more about understanding ingredients than it is actual technique. The more I cook, the more deeply I understand that less is always better. Fewer but better knife cuts, quicker more focused cooking applications, better ingredients presented in a natural state — a genuine respect of the glorious fresh foods that nature has provided, a respect that is one step closer to the truth.

This book is a celebration of those magnificent ingredients, the true heroes of Fresh cooking. It is also a reflection of where I am today, as curious and hungry as ever. Hungry to learn, hungry to push the conversation about our food supply forward, and hungry to share ideas. So if you take anything away from this book, I hope it will be an understanding of how vitally important it is to choose fresh ingredients when cooking for yourself and those you love.

Fresh is not just a sell-by date, it's a path toward a long and healthy life. Of course to get there, you need to make a conscious decision to eat fresh, and it's a choice you are up against at least two dozen times a day: fresh vs. processed. And the showdown between healthy, nutrient-packed, wholesome ingredients that have been simply prepared and so-called convenience foods is a battle we seem to be losing.

America eats 31 percent more packaged foods than any other country, everything from nondairy creamer and sweetened, stabilized salad dressings to frozen pizza and microwavable snacks. Nutritionisms, the glitzy claims touted by makers of packaged foods, speak directly to your desire to do the right thing for the health of yourself and your family. All those marketing dollars are effective. Natural foods — that is, foods your grandmother would recognize — are being stripped of their nutrients, vitamins, and fiber. The results are pink slime burgers and chicken nuggets shaped like dinosaurs vs. fresh ground beef and roasted chicken.

Ninety percent of the money America spends on food every day is spent on packaged and processed food — food that tastes good but is filled with fat, salt, and sugar and has very little nutritional value. It also makes us fat, gives us diabetes, high-blood pressure, and heart disease, and litters the planet with excessive packaging that takes centuries to decompose, yet we love it. A *lot* of it.

The end result? We're fat and we're sick. Our bodies are being exposed to chemicals and additives, unnatural lipids like trans-fats, and sodium levels many times higher than what exist in the natural world. Our bodies are not adapted to handle fast-acting carbohydrates like high-fructose corn syrup (HFCS), the supercheap, high-profit sweetener found in so many processed foods. Genetically modified foods such as corn, soybeans, peanuts, and wheat, once considered wholesome staples, are producing toxic and allergic reactions that human beings have never before experienced.

WHERE WE GOT OFF TRACK

HFCS, developed in Japan in 1966, was introduced into the U.S. marketplace around 1975, when the commodity price of raw sugar had soared 600 percent in just two years. This cheap sweetener was considered a huge advancement in biochemical science and an economic boon to the industrialized western world just getting its feet wet with modernized processed-food production. Food processors looking to stabilize their costs needed a reliable sugar substitute. In 1976 the U.S. Food and Drug Administration (FDA), with minimal clinical trials, classified HFCS as GRAS, generally recognized as safe.

After the green light from the FDA, it took about ten years for HFCS to deeply penetrate our food supply, just in time for the next wave of nutritional hyperbole. In 1982 the U.S. Department of Agriculture (USDA), the American

Medical Association, and the American Heart Association simultaneously recommended that we severely limit our intake of saturated fat based on a landmark study led by Minnesota epidemiologist Dr. Ancel Keys titled "The Seven Countries Study." The first of its kind in both size and scope, the study systematically examined the relationship between coronary heart disease and the lifestyle that encompassed what is now considered the high-fat "Western diet." The study, started in 1958, enlisted 12,763 men in seven countries and lasted for more than fifteen years. Its findings widely influenced the way Western doctors approached the control and prevention of cardiovascular disease. To a large degree, this new approach was successful; a paper published by the Centers for Disease Control (CDC) in August 1999 states a 56 percent drop in cardiovascular disease from 307 per 100,000 in 1950 to 134 per 100,000 in 1996. Although critics found holes in the Seven Countries Study, Dr. Keys landed on the cover of *Time* magazine on January 13, 1961.

As the consumer demand for low-fat food skyrocketed, food companies scrambled to reformulate their recipes using chemicals to approximate qualities like moisture, richness, and browning ability found in fat-rich foods. Food labels moved away from the simple recipes that had been perfected for generations, made with wholesome ingredients, to scientific formulations that superficially appeared the same but could now be labeled "fat free."

HFCS, already with a solid foot in the door of American food production, was a magical ingredient. If you replace fat with sugar, then balance it with salt and hydrogenated vegetable shortening, you get a result very similar in taste to traditional recipes and a product that fits into the USDA's suggested guidelines for "low fat" or "fat free," leading consumers to believe they were making a smart choice. A win-win, right?

WHAT WE KNOW NOW

The question that no one took the time to ask, including the FDA, is What are the long-term effects of these chemicals on the human body?

Between 1985 and 2010 America became the fattest nation on the planet, with 35.7 percent of adults in this country considered obese. Even more alarming, 12.5 million children are obese as well. The highest concentration of obesity also happens to be in the poorest parts of the country: the American South and the economically devastated factory towns of Ohio and Michigan. In 2012 the cost of the obesity epidemic was $190 billion, double what the government estimated, and it affects everything from gas consumption to insurance premiums.

But simply demonizing HFCS is not enough; to fully understand how we got off track—and how little the FDA actually knows about what is in our food supply—we need to examine what specific ingredients do to our body and how, over the years, their effects add up, one empty calorie at a time.

Sugar, in its natural, raw, organic state is not necessarily bad. It's when sugar is highly processed, and then hidden throughout our daily diet to the point that we don't even realize we're consuming it, that it becomes a serious problem.

There are many kinds of sugar: disaccharides like sucrose (table sugar), maltose (barley and hops in beer production), and lactose (milk sugar), and also monosaccharides such as glucose (simple carbohydrates like pasta, potatoes, and rice), fructose (fruit, berries, honey, and flowers), and galactose (less sweet than glucose and synthesized by the body, such as breast milk). They are all carbohydrates composed of carbon, hydrogen, and oxygen. Sugars are found in the tissues of most plants but are highly concentrated, enough for efficient extraction, in sugarcane, sugar beets, and corn.

In the plants our prehistoric ancestors would have gathered, concentrations of sugars were minimal because they contained lots of fiber and were naturally protected; what with blackberry thatches, bee hives, thick bamboolike sugarcane grass, it wasn't easy getting something sweet, which made the struggle to open a beehive, presumably with bare hands and sticks, worth it.

Today, in our modern life, we consume mostly glucose, sucrose, and fructose, all highly refined to improve accessibility, hitting the blood stream within minutes. Most doctors will agree that all sugar is bad. However, not all sugars are metabolized in the same way.

Glucose, a simple sugar found in pasta, potatoes, rice, and whole grains like quinoa, is your body's primary slow-burning source of energy. It stimulates the pancreas and increases your insulin level, signaling your brain to begin the process of telling you that you are full. If you are eating close to the source, by which I mean wholesome, unmanipulated ingredients like roasted potatoes with rosemary, garlic, good olive oil, and a little sea salt or whole wheat pasta loaded with vegetables and maybe a little protein like organic chicken or pork meatballs, the glucose you'll consume is full of fiber and easily digestible. Where it gets a little tricky is when the carb is stripped of any semblance of nutrition and fiber, as in frozen white-flour bagels, white-flour tortillas, pasta made with high-gluten bread flour, instant rice that has been cooked twice before you reheat it for the last five

TYLER FLORENCE FRESH

minutes—all seemingly innocuous foods you probably have in your kitchen.

Without the fiber to balance the hit of sugar, the glucose is not being slowly absorbed by your stomach, where it would turn into energy, but is instead processed in your liver, in the way alcohol is processed. This in turn raises your LDL (low-density lipoproteins). Over time, a poor diet that includes many refined carbs causes LDL to build up in your arteries, creating plaque, which has been linked to cardiovascular disease.

FRUCTOSE, HIGH-FRUCTOSE CORN SYRUP, AND SUCROSE

I'm grouping these together because they are basically the same: sucrose, extracted from sugarcane and sugar beets, is 50 percent fructose, HFCS and fructose, extracted from corn and fruit, are 55 percent fructose; the remaining percentages of both are glucose. The big difference among these is how they are metabolized by both the body and the brain. First, HFCS is only metabolized by the liver, not enzymes in the stomach. Once HFCS is processed through the liver, unless you exercise at an athletic level, your body starts to store it away as fat. Second, and this is most shocking to me, HFCS blocks your brain from receiving leptin, a hormone that regulates your nutrient intake. When you brain is satiated with nutrients, leptin says to your stomach, you've had enough.

Since HFCS is found throughout the entire food supply, it's hard to make a smart choice. The poorer the quality and the more processed the food, the more of it you actually have to eat to feel full. Not only are we consuming thousands of empty calories a day, but our bodies are also calling out for more, starved for nutrition. Once you become aware of HFCS, and the newest twist, crystalline fructose, which is even more refined at 98 percent fructose, you'll realize you can't get away from it—it is everywhere.

According to the CDC, Americans consume 60 pounds of HFCS per person, per year. With most Americans oblivious to food labels, the majority of that amount is consumed unknowingly. When you block the leptin signal from the stomach to the brain, consume a product labeled as two portions in one sitting, and do that two or three times a day for 365 days for ten years, you begin to see why we are so overweight. And this is just scratching the surface of the damage that highly refined sugars are doing to our bodies.

GMOS (GENETICALLY MODIFIED ORGANISMS)

The genetic modification, or genetic engineering, of plants and animals was made possible through the full identification of DNA in the 1950s. It took twenty years for the first direct human manipulation of an organism's genome to be used in modern DNA technology. In 1973 the first recombinant bacteria was created by expressing an exogenous gene salmonella from *E. coli*.

Today, recombinant DNA technology is at the core of most vibrant biotech companies and has produced mammoth breakthroughs in DNA sequencing, stem cell research, forensic science, the diagnosis of HIV, the hepatitis B vaccine, the production of synthesized insulin, and so on. Brilliant, life-saving work.

But nothing has generated more controversy than what is happening with recombinant DNA technology and our food supply and genetically modified food. It's a massive global industry and perhaps an even bigger business model. Through recombinant DNA technology, companies have successfully altered the gene structure of not only soybeans, but also cotton, wheat, corn, peanuts, alfalfa, and rice. This new generation of plants, all protected by patents (which legally bar farmers from saving seeds from their crops and replanting them the following year, a centuries-old practice), raises ethical concerns not only over who will own the food supply in the future, but also what testing has been done to protect the health of the general population.

How the FDA approves GMOs for general use is also of concern. To facilitate rapid approval, in 1990 the FDA along with the Food and Agriculture Organization, the World Health Organization, and biotech representatives conceived the "substantial equivalence" concept, which states that a novel food (GMOs, for example) should be considered the same as and as safe as conventional food if it demonstrates the same characteristics and composition as the conventional food, requiring no further investigation by the FDA of the long-term effects of human consumption or the environmental impact of producing the food.

The regulation of GMOs is overseen by three different government agencies: the Environmental Protection Agency evaluates GM plants for environmental safety; the USDA determines whether the plant is safe to grow; and the FDA says whether the plant is safe to eat. Under the current understanding of "substantial equivalence" a genetically modified ear of corn sold at a produce stand is not regulated because it is considered a "whole food," which falls under the USDA. The USDA oversees the widest area of regulation that covers drought-tolerant crops, disease-tolerant crops, crops grown for animal feed, and whole fruits, vegetables, and grains for human consumption. The FDA would test the ear of corn if it were processed into a cornflake, but the FDA's stance is that GM foods are substantially equivalent to unmodified "natural" foods and therefore not subject to FDA regulations.

Developed in 1992, the current FDA policy states that agri-biotech companies may voluntarily ask the FDA for a consultation. Companies working to create new GM foods are not required to consult the FDA, nor are they required to follow through with any recommendations by the FDA after the consultation. While many consumer groups and public safety organizations are pushing to have this become mandatory, the agency has countered by saying that the agency does not have the time, money, or resources to carry out such an exhaustive health and safety study of GM foods already in production.

Interestingly, while other countries such as Australia and Japan, and all twenty-seven of the EU countries, have decided to wait until GMO technology is fully tested and declared safe before introducing it into the general population, biotech companies are waiting for proof that GMOs are *un*safe—while these foods are undergoing no testing whatsoever.

As our global resources are depleted, companies holding key scientific advantages, in this case global patents, over our food supply, are going to control and some say hold hostage countries dependent on its product, a powerful incentive for agri-business to continue to modify—and patent—more and more elements of our food supply. Government regulations continue to favor these huge multinational corporations despite growing scientific evidence linking GM corn to organ damage and other GM crops to environmental devastation like global bee colony collapse.

The other side of the coin is the direct effects that GM foods are having on the food chain. If you are a parent like I am, you've noticed the alarming rate at which young children are developing allergies to not only peanuts, but to nuts in general. At the beginning of each school year, parents receive a letter forbidding nut products of any kind in school lunches or snacks. According to the CDC, in a study conducted in 2007, approximately 3 million children under the age of eighteen—approximately 3.9 percent of the population—reported having a food or digestive allergy in the previous twelve months. In the decade from 1996 to 2007 food allergies increased by 18 percent.

Of the eight types of food that account for more than 90 percent of all allergic reactions (milk, eggs, peanuts, tree nuts, fish, shellfish, soy, and wheat) several, including milk,

peanuts, tree nuts, fish, soy, and wheat, began to undergo genetic modification on a broad scale between 1994 and 1997. And although people have always had sensitivities to specific proteins in foods, allergies on this scale have never before been seen.

Allergies are just a quick snapshot; scientists in India, Japan, Canada, Russia, and the EU are looking for connections between environmental toxins and infertility, intestinal lesions, slow growth rates, damaged sperm cells, cancer, and more. Along with HFCS, these countries are studying DDT, lead, mercury, and bisphenol A—all once ignored by governments and regulatory agencies and now at the forefront of major health crises ranging from obesity to reproductive health, cancer, and autism.

GMOs represent one thing only and that's control. There is no scientific proof that farmers produce more crops with GMOs than with conventional seeds and methods, including organic farming. Yet we are facing the biggest change to our food supply in ten thousand years of history, all without our knowledge or consent. Meanwhile, we are the fattest country on the planet with the highest cancer rate. We also have the second-highest infant mortality rate in the Western world. Our food supply is tainted and is killing us. At this point, there is just no other position to argue, unless of course you are in a position to make a profit from that very food supply.

A FRESH ECONOMIC PERSPECTIVE

Our ability to compete in a global, free-market society is only as strong as our population is healthy—not propped up on medication but legitimately healthy. In 2012 health care and medical expenses in the United States exceed $2 trillion, ten times the $256 billion spent on health care in 1980. The dramatic increase in health care costs and the decline of the health of the American population coincide with the rise of the biotech industry. The USDA invests in GMOs with billions of dollars in tax incentives and subsidies handed out to industrial farms willing to plant them. The largest slice of the subsidy pie, $17 billion, goes to develop food additives like corn syrup, high-fructose corn syrup, cornstarch, rice, and soy oils. The vast majority of produce subsidized by the USDA ends up in junk food, while a mere $261 million goes to subsidize healthier foods like fruits and vegetables. Organic farms get nothing.

Instead, organic farmers have to navigate seemingly endless red tape and pay fees to prove that their farms are pure, while factory farms go through zero FDA inspection and get government assistance to produce low-quality food that's killing us. We must all wake up to the fact that cheaper is not better. The subsidies and tax incentives provided to large factory farms create an uneven playing field that drives down the cost of the poorest-quality foods on our grocery-store shelves, thus creating the illusion that conventional and organic foods are too expensive, when in fact they reflect what food should really cost. Farmers doing the right thing, providing densely nutritious foods, are being forced out of the market.

I hope all of this makes you angry. It's intended to. We humans are a hardy lot, we've been around for a long time, doing just fine up until the past twenty to thirty years. The government wants to blame it all on us, claiming we're fat because of the choices we make. I want to tell you that it's not exactly true. You are a product of your environment. Companies don't care about you or your children as much as they care about your money. They want you to remain uninformed and continue to consume their products. If you get sick from what they sell, it's your fault.

But you don't have to accept this state of affairs. Rethink how investing in food is investing in your own health and the health of your family. Don't take marketing at face value. It's up to you to read labels and everything you can get your hands on about health and nutrition, to insist on transparency, and most important, to eat *fresh*.

Together we can make a difference.

WHERE DO WE GO FROM HERE?

The way I see it, food is fuel. If we think about the food we eat this way, we would all be a lot healthier. You know it and I know it. It's time to change the conversation from gluttony to satiation, our daily diet from fattening to fresh. It's not about how much we eat, but how *well* we eat. With this book, I would love to help you see that nutritious meals can also be delicious. To that end, *Fresh* is full of simple ways to

transform healthy ingredients into absolute showstoppers. This book represents an evolution from what I've written in the past, with new plating techniques, flavor combinations, and a philosophy of food that has been influenced by my new roots in California and honed over the years that I've been cooking in restaurants and for the viewers of my shows. I have come to believe that you are only as healthy as the food you put in your body. That said, there is a universe of food that we can explore and cook together that goes well beyond a bowl of salad.

To understand the full scope of this book, you'll have to get your hands dirty and cook something. Wash off the soil of generation-old ideas, open your mind, and really see food for its natural beauty. This book isn't about organic and sustainable per se, it's about making the choice to feed yourself and your family fresh, wholesome food. To make that point as strongly as I can I have organized the recipes by ingredient rather than a more conventional soups, salads, entrées, desserts breakdown. I hope it will encourage you to be inspired by what looks great in the market rather than approach a meal or menu with a preconceived notion of what you'd like to cook. Each recipe features one "hero" ingredient—the one element without which the dish would not have the same character. Every other element is open to your interpretation, whether you want to swap out the protein—substituting another firm white fish for a halibut fillet or a grilled chicken breast for a pan-seared pork chop— or use a seasonal fruit or vegetable you just couldn't pass up for the one I've called for. Let your eyes and your stomach be your guide and mix and match the components as you see fit.

The point is to put fresh first. This entire book is about fresh—fresh ideas on how to make your tongue happy, a fresh perspective on nutrition, fresh dynamic flavors, a fresh approach to cooking techniques, and most important, a healthy decision to put fresh *first*.

FRESH RECIPES

WHITE SPANISH ANCHOVIES, HEARTS OF PALM, QUAIL EGGS, AND LEMON AIOLI

SERVES 4

LEMON AIOLI
2 egg whites
½ teaspoon Dijon mustard
1 tablespoon grated lemon zest
1 cup grapeseed oil, or more as needed
¼ teaspoon kosher salt
Freshly cracked black pepper
¼ teaspoon sugar
½ teaspoon fresh lemon juice

CHILE OIL
4 to 5 serrano chiles
1 cup extra-virgin olive oil
Kosher salt

1 (14.25-ounce) can hearts of palm, drained
1 celery heart, split into bite-size pieces
8 fresh quail eggs
2 to 3 tablespoons white vinegar

FRIED PARSLEY
¾ cup all-purpose flour
¼ cup cornstarch
½ teaspoon kosher salt
1 egg white
¾ cup ice-cold club soda
Canola oil, for deep frying
12 sprigs flat-leaf parsley
Kosher salt

20 marinated fresh Spanish anchovies
½ teaspoon dried red pepper flakes
Flaky sea salt

Make the lemon aioli. In a blender, combine the egg whites, mustard, and lemon zest. Blend until smooth. With the blender running on low speed, add the grapeseed oil in a slow, steady stream. Continue to blend until emulsified and creamy. Add the salt, pepper, sugar, and lemon juice, then pulse a couple of times until combined. Refrigerate until ready to use.

Make the chile oil. Split the chiles lengthwise and place in a small saucepan. Add the olive oil and season lightly with salt. Slowly warm over low-medium heat, bringing almost to a simmer, for 15 to 20 minutes. (Do not let the oil bubble.) Once the chiles are warmed through, remove them from the heat and allow to steep in the oil until completely cool. Strain the oil and discard the chiles.

Finely slice 2 or 3 hearts of palm into thin rounds. Then slice 2 hearts of palm lengthwise. Finely slice the celery into thin crescents. Place the celery in a bowl of ice water and chill in the fridge for 10 to 15 minutes to crisp up.

Boil the quail eggs. Fill a large pot with 3 to 4 inches of cold water, and add the vinegar and the eggs (the vinegar helps to soften the shells and makes them easier to peel). Bring to a boil over high heat. Cook for 5 minutes, stirring, from the moment the water starts boiling. Allow to cool, then peel the eggs and halve them lengthwise.

Fry the parsley. In a large mixing bowl, combine the flour, cornstarch, and salt. Make a well in the center and add the egg white. Using a whisk, lightly whip the egg white until foamy. Then gradually pour in the club soda while continuing to whisk. With the whisk, work your way from the center out to slowly incorporate the dry ingredients and form a smooth, lump-free batter. Heat 2 to 3 inches of canola oil to 350°F in a large pot. Dip the parsley sprigs in the batter, shake off any excess, then fry until crispy and lightly golden, about 2 minutes. Drain on paper towels and season with salt while hot.

To assemble, arrange the hearts of palm, and celery on plates. Place 5 or so anchovies on each plate with the quail egg halves. Garnish with the fried parsley. Drizzle with the chile oil, dot with aioli, and sprinkle with the red pepper flakes and flaky sea salt.

anchovies

Much of the fish population off the coasts of the United States is on the verge of collapse, from Cod, Atlantic salmon, and flounder to sea bass, porgy, and grouper off the Atlantic coast to chinook salmon, petrale sole, and halibut off the Pacific Coast. The fish aren't suffering from a lack of food; the ocean has enough food for everyone on the planet. It's the inefficient and antiquated techniques we use to fish our waters that are killing our ecosystem. Looking across the entire food web of the ocean, we burn more calories, both human and in fossil fuels, harvesting and processing some species of fish than the fish provides as food, a downward slope that will lead to complete oceanic collapse.

Seafood is classified on a trophic scale, which represents the succession of organisms that eat other organisms and then in turn are eaten themselves (the food chain). Level 1 is phytoplankton (algae and flora). Level 2 is zooplankton (krill and small shrimp). Level 3 is forage species (anchovies, sardines, market squid). Levels 4 and 5 are the predators that consume the entire chain. By fishing at only the highest trophic level (tuna, salmon, halibut, shark) we consume the entire ecosystem. The biomass energy transfer that happens along the trophic index is where we lose valuable calories and waste enormous amounts of both human and fossil energy.

For example, bluefin tuna, which is 4.21 out of 5 on the trophic scale, has to consume 1,622 calories for every one it provides, whereas anchovies, which are only 2.9 on the trophic scale, consume just 79 calories for every one they produce. Bringing an average price of three to six cents a pound, however, most of the anchovy catch never gets consumed by humans: 90 percent of it is used for fish meal in pet food or as bait for larger fish. A sizable portion of the fish meal goes to feed farmed salmon, which consume 8 to 9 pounds of fish meal to produce every pound of consumable salmon.

Food lower on the scale is easier to harvest and much more abundant. If we make these forage fish sexy, fishermen can get a better price per pound, and they'll be too expensive to use for pet food, too prized to be bait. The anchovy would become a truly sustainable fish that happens to be delicious, is packed with healthy omega-3 fats, and contains almost zero mercury. Should we ever eat tuna again? Sure, once or twice a year, when it's in season.

BROCCOLI AND ANCHOVY BAGNA CAUDA WITH PARMESAN

SERVES 4 TO 6

1 bunch broccoli (about 1 pound)
1 bunch broccolini
Extra-virgin olive oil
Kosher salt and freshly cracked black pepper

BAGNA CAUDA
½ cup clarified butter (see Note)
½ cup extra-virgin olive oil
15 fresh white anchovy fillets in oil (boquerones)
2 Calabrian chiles packed in oil
3 garlic cloves, very thinly sliced
¼ cup roasted cashews
3 tablespoons golden raisins, plumped
   in warm water
Freshly cracked black pepper

⅓ cup finely shaved Parmigiano-Reggiano
Freshly cracked black pepper

Prepare the broccoli. Preheat the oven to 425°F. Wash the broccoli and discard the tough stem. Cut into florets. Separate the broccolini into individual stems, reserving some of the smaller leaves and flowers for garnish. Arrange the broccoli and broccolini pieces on a baking sheet, drizzle with olive oil, and season with salt and pepper. Roast in the oven for 18 to 20 minutes, until the broccoli is becoming charred and crisp around the edges.

Make the bagna cauda. Warm the clarified butter and olive oil in a large sauté pan over medium heat. Add the anchovies, red chiles, and garlic and heat gently for 7 to 8 minutes. This will allow the flavors to infuse. Add the cashews and raisins and toss together. Season with black pepper (no salt is required, as there's enough salt in the anchovies already).

Arrange the roasted broccoli on a large platter. Pour the bagna cauda over the broccoli. Finish with the shaved Parmesan and a few turns of cracked black pepper. Garnish with the reserved raw broccolini leaves and flowers.

NOTE To clarify butter, melt ½ cup (1 stick) unsalted butter in a small saucepan over medium-low heat. When completely melted, skim the surface, discarding the white foam, then carefully pour off the clarified butter, leaving any milk solids behind. The clarified butter has a higher smoking point than butter containing milk solids.

WHITE CHEDDAR GOUGÈRE, APPLE PULP, PROSCIUTTO, AND SAGE

MAKES 35 TO 40 GOUGÈRES

GOUGÈRES

½ cup (1 stick) unsalted butter
½ teaspoon kosher salt
1 cup all-purpose flour
4 large eggs
1 cup grated sharp white Cheddar

APPLE

6 Honeycrisp apples
2 tablespoons unsalted butter
¼ teaspoon ground allspice
¼ teaspoon ground cinnamon
¼ teaspoon ground cardamom
Pinch ground cloves
1 tablespoon orange blossom honey
Juice of 1 lemon

Extra-virgin olive oil
¼ bunch sage, leaves only
10 to 15 thin slices prosciutto,
    torn into bite-size pieces
Fleur de sel
Freshly cracked black pepper

Make the gougères. Preheat the oven to 425°F and line 2 baking sheets with parchment paper or silicone mats. In a large saucepan, combine the butter, salt, and 1 cup of water. Stir over high heat until the butter melts completely. Then remove the pan from the heat and add all the flour at once. Stir vigorously with a wooden spoon until smooth, then transfer to a mixer fitted with a paddle attachment. Beat on medium speed, adding the eggs one at a time and ensuring that each egg is fully incorporated before adding the next. Beat in the grated cheese.

Transfer the dough to a pastry bag, or use two wet spoons, to drop neat 1-tablespoon mounds on the prepared baking sheets, spacing them about an inch apart. Bake for 25 to 30 minutes, until golden and crisp. Turn the oven off and let the gougères dry out in the oven with the door ajar to keep them nice and crisp.

Cook the apples. Peel the apples and discard the cores. Cut into ½-inch dice. Melt the butter in a large sauté pan over high heat. When it is foaming, add the spices; they will toast instantly and become fragrant. Add the apples and sauté for 3 to 4 minutes, until browned. Add 2 tablespoons of water, the honey, and the lemon juice. Cook for 3 to 4 minutes, until the liquid is reduced and the apples are tender. Set aside to cool.

Set a clean sauté pan over medium heat. Add enough olive oil to coat the pan, and when it is hot, fry the sage leaves until crisp and almost transparent, about 1 minute. Drain on paper towels. Add the prosciutto pieces to the same pan in a single layer (work in batches if necessary). Cook for 1 minute on each side to crisp them up. Drain on paper towels.

To assemble, carefully tear off the top third of each gougère and spoon in some warm apple filling. Top with the sage and prosciutto, and season lightly with fleur de sel. Drizzle each plate with olive oil and sprinkle with cracked black pepper.

ROASTED APPLES, POTATOES, AND BRUSSELS SPROUTS WITH WHIPPED PARMESAN

SERVES 4 TO 6

2 medium Pink Lady or Gala apples
1 pound assorted baby creamer potatoes
    (Red Bliss, gold, purple)
1 pound Brussels sprouts
2 tablespoons extra-virgin olive oil, plus more
    for serving
8 to 10 fresh sage leaves
Kosher salt and freshly cracked black pepper
½ cup crème fraîche
¼ cup grated Parmigiano-Reggiano

Make the apples and vegetables. Preheat the oven to 500°F. Set a large cast-iron pan in the oven to get good and hot. Cut each apple into 8 wedges and remove the cores. Cut the potatoes in half, and cut the Brussels sprouts in half through the stem.

Remove the pan from the oven and add the olive oil. Add the sage leaves and let them sizzle for 30 to 40 seconds to crisp up the leaves and infuse the oil. Remove the leaves from the oil, drain on paper towels, and set aside for garnish. Add the apples, potatoes, and sprouts to the hot pan, season with salt and pepper, and toss to coat everything. Return the pan to the oven and roast for 15 to 20 minutes, until the potatoes are tender.

Make the Parmesan whip. In a large mixing bowl, combine the crème fraîche, Parmesan, and salt and pepper. Whisk together to aerate and thicken, then refrigerate to chill and firm.

When the vegetables are done, remove the pan from the oven and allow to cool slightly. Then dollop spoonfuls of whipped Parmesan crème fraîche on top so it melts over the vegetables and forms a sauce. Garnish with cracked black pepper, the fried sage leaves, and a drizzle of extra-virgin olive oil.

GRILLED ARTICHOKES WITH ANCHOVY MAYO AND CUCUMBER-LEMON SALSA

SERVES 4

QUICK PICKLED LEMON
2 lemons
2 teaspoons yellow mustard seeds
½ cup sugar
½ cup apple cider vinegar
Pinch kosher salt
2 or 3 fennel fronds

ARTICHOKES
1 lemon, cut in half
4 sprigs fresh thyme
2 garlic cloves
2 or 3 black peppercorns
1 bay leaf
1 cup dry white wine
4 artichokes
Extra-virgin olive oil
Kosher salt and freshly cracked black pepper

ANCHOVY MAYO
2 egg whites
6 oil-packed anchovy fillets
½ teaspoon Dijon mustard
1 teaspoon roasted garlic (see Note)
2 teaspoons fresh lemon juice
1 cup grapeseed oil
Kosher salt and freshly cracked black pepper

CUCUMBER-LEMON SALSA
1 cup peeled and diced hothouse cucumber
⅓ cup lightly packed pickled lemon
1 Thai bird chile, finely sliced
Extra-virgin olive oil
Kosher salt

Fresh tarragon leaves
Fresh flat-leaf parsley

Pickle the lemons. Cut the lemons into thin slices. Combine the mustard seeds, sugar, ½ cup of water, and the vinegar in a pot set over high heat. Bring to a simmer, then remove from the heat. Add the salt. Arrange the lemon slices flat in a vacuum-seal bag. Place the fennel fronds on top of the lemons, then pour the pickling mixture into the bag. Seal the bag on the highest pressure setting. Once the vacuum seal has taken, the lemons are ready to use.

Make the artichokes. In a large pot, heat 3 quarts of water over high heat. Add the lemon halves, thyme, garlic, peppercorns, bay leaf, and white wine. Bring to a simmer. Drop the artichokes into the water and cover with a round of parchment paper, which will ensure the artichokes stay submerged. Simmer for 12 to 15 minutes, until just tender but still firm. Drain, and cut the artichokes in half lengthwise. Use a small spoon to scrape out the inedible fibers, then drizzle with a little olive oil and season with salt and pepper. Preheat a grill or grill pan. Grill over medium heat, about 5 minutes on the cut side and 1 minute on the other side.

Make the anchovy mayo. In a blender, combine the egg whites, anchovies, mustard, garlic, and lemon juice. Blend until smooth. With the blender running, add the grapeseed oil in a slow, steady stream so the mixture emulsifies. Season with salt and plenty of freshly cracked black pepper. Mix well. Refrigerate until ready to use.

Make the cucumber-lemon salsa. Place the diced cucumber in a vacuum-seal bag and seal on high pressure. Leave to sit for 10 to 15 minutes. Chop the pickled lemon. In a bowl, mix the lemon, cucumber, and sliced chile. Dress with a little olive oil and season with salt.

Place some anchovy mayo in the cavity of each grilled artichoke and top with a big scoop of cucumber-lemon salsa. Garnish with fresh tarragon and parsley.

NOTE To roast garlic, cut the top off a head of garlic to expose the cloves. Place on a sheet of foil, drizzle with olive oil, and season with salt. Fold the edges of the foil together to create a sealed pouch. Roast in a 350°F oven for 25 to 30 minutes. When cool, squeeze out the roasted pulp as needed or store in the refrigerator for 3 to 4 days.

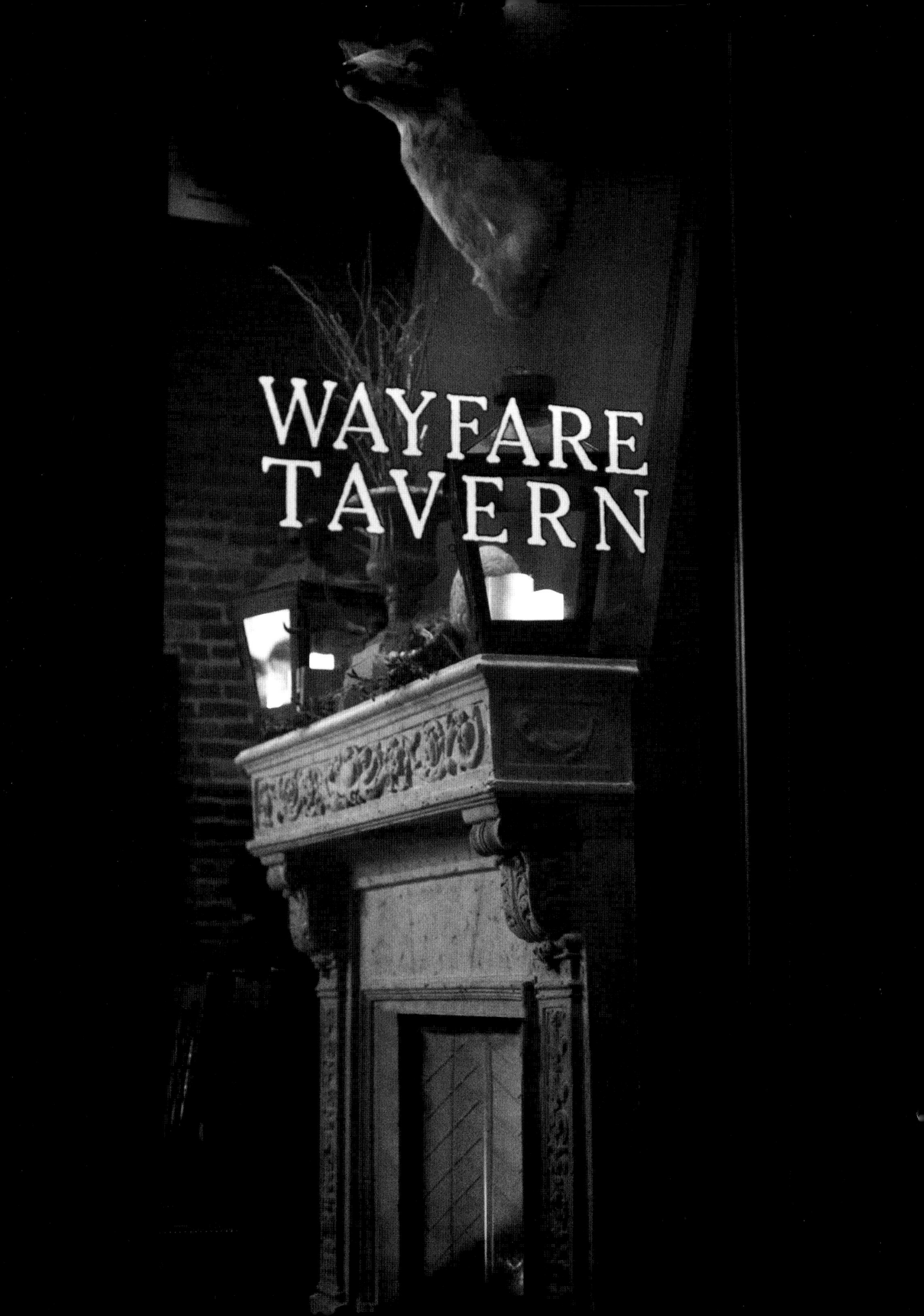
WAYFARE
TAVERN

ASPARAGUS
GRILLED CHEESE WITH POACHED EGG AND GREENS

SERVES 4

To preserve the aroma, don't make the truffle mayonnaise more than an hour in advance.

TRUFFLE MAYONNAISE

2 egg whites
½ teaspoon Dijon mustard
2 teaspoons fresh lemon juice
¼ teaspoon kosher salt
¼ teaspoon sugar
1 cup grapeseed oil
1 ounce fresh black truffle shavings or
    1½ teaspoons truffle oil

24 asparagus spears, woody ends trimmed
8 slices (about ½ inch thick) buttermilk or
    sourdough bread
3 to 4 ounces Mt. Tam triple-cream cheese,
    cut into ⅛-inch-thick slices
Kosher salt and freshly cracked black pepper
1 tablespoon white vinegar
4 large eggs
Extra-virgin olive oil, for grilling sandwiches
1 pint assorted greens and sprouts

NOTE Try growing your own sprouts at home. Soak seeds (such as radish, alfalfa, clover, broccoli) in water to cover for about 8 hours. Rinse, and spread evenly on a dampened piece of cheesecloth or paper towel set in a flat dish. Place in a sheltered but sunny, warm place. Moisten the cheesecloth with fresh water each morning and evening until the seeds begin to sprout.

Make the mayonnaise. Combine the egg whites, mustard, lemon juice, salt, and sugar in a blender. Blend until smooth. With the blender running, add the grapeseed oil in a slow, steady stream and blend until the mixture emulsifies. Remove about ¾ cup of the mayo and reserve for another use. Add the truffles or truffle oil and blend again until smooth. Refrigerate in a sealed container until ready to use.

Cook the asparagus. Bring a large pot of salted water to a boil. Cook the asparagus for 1 to 2 minutes, until tender and bright green. Drain the asparagus and transfer to a bowl of salted ice water. Leave to cool for 1 minute, then drain and set aside.

Assemble the sandwiches. Smear each slice of bread with some truffle mayonnaise. Top 4 of the slices with a slice of cheese, followed by a neat layer of asparagus spears arranged ½ inch apart, trimming the asparagus so they fit nicely on the bread. Season with salt and pepper, then place the remaining slice of bread on top, mayonnaise-side down.

Poach the eggs. Fill a medium saucepan with 3 to 4 inches of water and bring to a boil over medium-high heat. Reduce to a simmer and add the vinegar. Working with 1 egg at a time, crack an egg into a small bowl. Stir the water with a wooden spoon to create a whirlpool, then gently slide the egg into the center. The circulating water will cause the white to neatly envelop the yolk and yield a perfectly poached egg. Cook at a gentle simmer for 3 to 4 minutes, until the white sets and the egg is just firm enough to handle but still tender. Use a slotted spoon to remove, and drain well on a paper towel.

Grill the sandwiches. Drizzle the sandwiches on both sides with a little olive oil. Grill in a panini press for 2 to 3 minutes on medium-high heat (or 2 to 3 minutes per side in a nonstick skillet) until they are golden brown and the cheese is melted. Use a serrated knife to carefully cut each sandwich into individual finger-size portions, cutting between the asparagus spears. Serve the poached eggs with the grilled sandwich pieces immediately. Garnish with the greens and serve with dots of truffle mayonnaise.

asparagus

Don't forget to eat your asparagus. Today in America there are 5.4 million people with Alzheimer's disease. Although there is no known cure for this progressive brain disease, a study by the National Institute on Aging suggests that changes in diet can significantly reduce an adult's risk of developing Alzheimer's. The study shows that a deficiency of folate, or folic acid, a vitamin B complex, can deplete the body of choline and increase the toxicity level of beta-amyloids in the brain. (Beta-amyloids are a protein fragment suspected to be one cause of Alzheimer's.) Choline helps to maintain cell membrane structure and aids in the development of neurotransmitters, which facilitate communication among the brain cells. Asparagus happens to have one of the highest folate levels of any vegetable: 5.3 ounces (about a cup) provides 66 percent of your daily recommendation. Not only rich in folate, asparagus is a true superfood and a nutritional powerhouse. It's packed with vitamin K for strong bones, antioxidants that repair damage done by free radicals, and vitamins A, C, and E, the latter also known as "the sex vitamin" that helps stimulate androgen and estrogen to raise your libido.

ASPARAGUS, SWEET PEAS, AND FAVAS, BURRATA, AND GRILLED SOURDOUGH

SERVES 4

GREEN VEGETABLE PESTO

1 pound asparagus, trimmed and cut into
    ½-inch pieces
1 cup green beans cut in ½-inch pieces
1 cup English peas, fresh or frozen
1 cup shelled and peeled fava beans
½ cup toasted pine nuts, plus extra for garnish
½ cup grated Parmigiano-Reggiano
¼ cup extra-virgin olive oil
Kosher salt and freshly cracked black pepper

1 small sourdough loaf
Extra-virgin olive oil
2 balls (about 8 ounces each) fresh burrata cheese
Flaky sea salt
½ lemon
Fresh pea tendrils

Make the pesto. Bring a large pot of water to a boil and salt it generously. Add the asparagus, green beans, peas, and favas, and blanch for 3 minutes. Drain in a colander, then immediately transfer the veggies to a large bowl of salted ice water. When they are cool, drain again. Then spread them on a clean kitchen towel and pat dry. Place all but ½ cup of the blanched vegetables in a food processor, and add the pine nuts, Parmesan, and olive oil. Puree for 5 minutes, scraping down the sides once or twice until completely smooth. Season with salt and pepper.

Make the toasts. Preheat a grill or grill pan. Cut the sourdough loaf into ½-inch-thick slices. Drizzle with a little olive oil and grill over high heat until charred and crispy, about 2 minutes per side.

Spread the burrata on the slices of grilled sourdough. Serve the vegetable pesto on the side, topped with the reserved ½ cup blanched vegetables. Finish with sea salt, a drizzle of olive oil, a squeeze of lemon juice, the toasted pine nuts, and pea tendrils.

ORGANIC CHICKEN, ISRAELI COUSCOUS, AND **BASIL** BROTH

This cut, with breastbone and ribs removed but skin and wing joint attached, is called the "airline" cut.

CHICKEN

2 boneless chicken breast halves with skin
    and wing "drumette" attached
2 sprigs fresh thyme
2 sprigs fresh rosemary
4 thin lemon slices
Kosher salt and freshly cracked black pepper
2 tablespoons extra-virgin olive oil
2 tablespoons unsalted butter

COUSCOUS

Kosher salt
Squeeze of fresh lemon juice
1 pound Israeli couscous
1 tablespoon extra-virgin olive oil

PESTO

4 cups lightly packed fresh basil leaves
1 cup lightly packed flat-leaf parsley
1 cup finely ground Parmigiano-Reggiano
1 garlic clove, grated
1 tablespoon fresh lemon juice
½ cup extra-virgin olive oil

1 tablespoon unsalted butter
Fresh basil buds
½ cup shaved Parmigiano-Reggiano

Make the chicken. Place the breast halves in separate vacuum-seal bags and add a sprig of thyme, a sprig of rosemary, and 2 lemon slices to each one. Season with salt and pepper, and add a tablespoon of olive oil to each bag. Seal the bags and place in a water bath held at a consistent 65°C (149°F) for 1 hour to cook sous vide. (See page 33 for more on sous vide cooking.) Remove the bags from the water.

Make the couscous. Bring 3 cups of water to a boil in a medium pot. Season with salt and the lemon juice. Then add the couscous and olive oil and cook until tender, 6 to 7 minutes. The liquid will not be completely absorbed; do not drain.

Make the pesto. In a blender, combine the basil, parsley, Parmesan, garlic, lemon juice, and olive oil and puree until smooth.

Remove the chicken from the vacuum bags and pat dry. Season with salt and pepper. Melt the 2 tablespoons butter in a medium sauté pan over medium-high heat. Add the chicken skin-side down and sear until the skin is crispy and golden, 3 minutes.

Fold the pesto into the warm couscous—it will turn bright green. Season with salt and the 1 tablespoon butter. Serve the chicken with the couscous, and garnish with fresh basil buds and the shaved Parmesan.

sous vide

From the time I began cooking in the mid-1980s I've seen plenty of culinary movements come and go. I think it's safe to say that we are now living in a postmolecular world. Molecular gastronomy is exciting from a professional point of view, but being a naturalist, especially when it comes to cooking, I'm glad to see a focus on ingredients in their purity replacing manipulation of ingredients just for the sake of novelty. However, of the many cooking techniques that were developed or widely integrated in the past decade, sous vide is one that will stand the test of time. In a sense, it already has. Originally described in 1799, sous vide (literally "under vacuum") entails cooking foods in an airtight container at very low temperatures. The technique was adapted for restaurant use at Jean and Pierre Troisgros's legendary La Maison Troisgros in Roanne, France, in 1974 and is now used by chefs around the world.

The results are outstanding. From a flavor standpoint, nothing is lost during sous vide cooking. When you roast a chicken, flavorful fat and juices collect in the bottom of the roasting pan; when you poach chicken in water, the broth may taste amazing but the chicken itself is incredibly bland. When the same chicken is vacuum-sealed and poached at 140°F using a machine that regulates the water temperature precisely, the flavor has nowhere to go.

Vacuum sealers are very easy to come by, and you can pick up a small tabletop water bath unit that will maintain a consistent water temperature for a few hundred dollars. However, even without the equipment it's simple to approximate the effect at home: Either vacuum seal cuts of meat and seasonings in a food storage bag, or wrap them very tightly in plastic. Heat a large pot of water to roughly 140°F and clip a candy thermometer on the side of the pot. Submerge the wrapped meat and cook, adjusting the heat as needed to keep the water temperature at 140°F. Have a bowl of ice handy to cool down the water bath if the temperature starts to climb. Chicken breasts take about 45 minutes, pork tenderloin about an hour. Carefully remove the meat from the water and allow it to cool slightly. The last step is to sear the chicken or pork in a sauté pan with a small amount of butter or olive oil to caramelize and brown the surface.

chlorophyll,
the foundation of life

The process of plant photosynthesis starts a reaction that is the absolute beginning of the food chain that ends with what's on your dinner plate. Organisms that do not get their energy directly from the sun get their energy either by eating organisms that do (i.e., plants) or by eating organisms that eat plants. We humans lose out nutritionally when we eat animals that eat plants rather than eat enough of the plants themselves. Here's why: For every calorie that plants consume through natural sunlight, they provide one calorie of nutrition, a conversion rate of 1:1, which is an extremely efficient method of food production. In stark contrast, grain-fed cattle must consume thirty-five calories for every calorie their beef provides in nutrition. By eating primarily at the top of the food chain, we are nutritionally in the red. By shifting plants to the forefront of what we consume, we could easily and efficiently feed the world.

Perhaps even more important is the nutrition provided by a plant-focused diet. Green foods that contain chlorophyll supply more nutrition for the lowest number of calories than any food on the planet.

Chlorophyll's molecular makeup is similar to that of our own blood. Both have carbon, hydrogen, oxygen, and nitrogen surrounding a single atom; the difference is that chlorophyll's nucleus is magnesium and hemoglobin's nucleus is iron. Scientists often refer to rich chlorophyll as the "blood" of plants, and it has the power to regenerate our bodies at the molecular and cellular levels. It cleanses the blood and helps regenerate red blood cells, enabling the body to carry more oxygen and remove more toxins. Chlorophyll is very alkaline and can help lower your body's overall pH, which creates a domino effect of reduced inflammation and a lower risk of cancer—not to mention it's a delicious vitamin- and mineral-packed powerhouse.

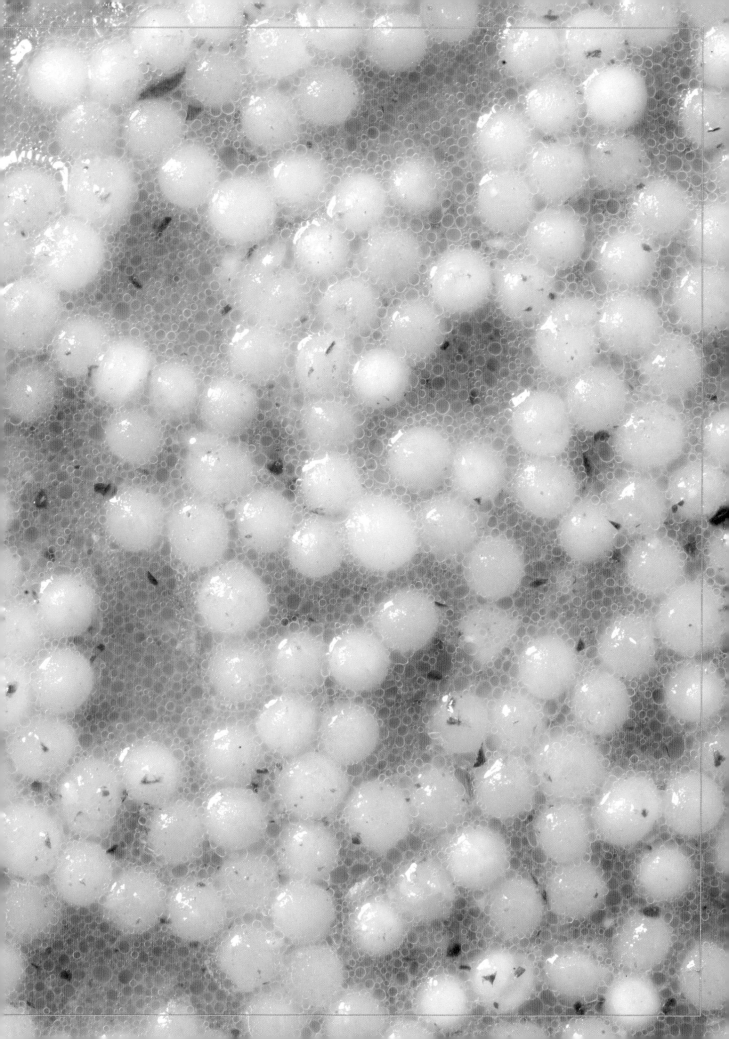

SUMMER BEAN SALAD WITH SMOKED TROUT AND PASTINA

SERVES 4 TO 6

PASTINA
2 cups pastina
Extra-virgin olive oil

LEMON AIOLI
2 egg whites
¼ teaspoon Dijon mustard
2 tablespoons fresh lemon juice
½ teaspoon grated lemon zest
¼ teaspoon kosher salt
¼ teaspoon sugar
1 cup grapeseed oil

TOMATOES
1 quart olive oil
3 cups mixed cherry and grape tomatoes
   (red, yellow, orange)
1 tablespoon fresh lemon juice
Kosher salt and freshly cracked black pepper

BEANS
1 pound haricots verts or thin green beans
½ pound yellow wax beans

4 smoked trout fillets
2 tablespoons fresh chervil sprigs

Toast the pastina. Bring 2½ cups of water to a boil. Place the pastina in a large heatproof bowl, and add the boiling water. Cover and let stand for 10 minutes until the pastina is fully bloomed and has absorbed all the liquid. Heat a little olive oil in a large sauté pan, and toast the pastina for 2 to 3 minutes, tossing frequently.

Make the lemon aioli. In a blender, blend the egg whites until just foamy. Add the mustard, lemon juice, lemon zest, salt, and sugar. With the blender running, add the grapeseed oil in a slow, steady stream so the mixture emulsifies. Chill until ready to use.

Prepare the tomatoes. Heat the olive oil to 350°F in a large Dutch oven. Drop the tomatoes into a basket or strainer, and submerge it in the hot oil for 4 to 5 seconds, until the tomatoes just pop. Remove and set aside. Transfer ¼ cup of the cooking oil to a small bowl and whisk in the lemon juice to make a cherry tomato vinaigrette. Season with salt and pepper.

Cook the beans. Bring a large pot of salted water to a boil. Add the beans and cook until just al dente, 3 to 4 minutes. Drain, submerge in a large bowl of salted ice water until cooled, then drain well. Dress the beans lightly with some of the lemon aioli.

Carefully break the trout into large flakes. Arrange the beans on a serving platter and top with the cherry tomatoes. Scatter with the toasted pastina and flaked trout pieces. Dot with more of the lemon aioli, drizzle the plate with some of the cherry tomato vinaigrette, and garnish with the fresh chervil.

SWEET PEA FALAFEL, CHARRED CORN, AND PINK CHILE MAYO

SERVES 4

SWEET PEA FALAFEL

2 cups dried green split peas, soaked in
    water overnight
1 teaspoon baking powder
1 small onion, coarsely chopped
4 garlic cloves, smashed
1 tablespoon cumin seeds, toasted and ground
1 tablespoon toasted coriander seeds
¼ teaspoon dried red pepper flakes
2 handfuls flat-leaf parsley leaves,
    coarsely chopped
1 handful fresh cilantro leaves, coarsely chopped
Kosher salt and freshly cracked black pepper
Vegetable oil, for deep frying

PINK CHILE MAYO

½ cup mayonnaise
½ cup sour cream
1 teaspoon red chile sauce, such as Sriracha
½ teaspoon honey
1 teaspoon fresh lemon juice
Kosher salt and freshly cracked black pepper

CHARRED CORN

2 ears fresh corn
Kosher salt and freshly cracked black pepper

SWEET PEA PUREE

2 cups fresh English peas
Kosher salt

Mâche
Breakfast radish, thinly sliced
Flaky sea salt
Extra-virgin olive oil

Make the falafel. Drain the split peas and put them in a food processor and pulse to coarsely grind. Add the baking powder, onion, garlic, spices, and herbs; process until the mixture is smooth, scraping down the sides of the bowl as needed. Taste, and season with salt and pepper. Refrigerate until ready to fry the falafel.

Make the pink chile mayo. In a large bowl, combine the mayonnaise, sour cream, chile sauce, honey, lemon juice, and salt and pepper. Stir well and refrigerate until ready to use.

Make the corn. Heat a grill or grill pan until very hot. Shuck the corn and char it well on all sides, about 12 minutes total. Cool the corn slightly, and then use a sharp knife to slice off the kernels. Season with salt and pepper.

Make the sweet pea puree. In a small saucepan, combine the peas and ¼ cup of water. Cover and cook over high heat for 3 to 4 minutes, until the peas are bright green. Place the peas and the steaming water in a blender and puree until completely smooth. Season lightly with salt.

Fry the falafel. Pour 3 inches of vegetable oil into a deep, heavy pot and set over medium-high heat; heat to 375°F. Use two spoons to form the falafel mixture into quenelles, using about 1 heaping tablespoon for each. Carefully slip 4 or 5 falafel at a time into the hot oil. Fry until crispy and golden on all sides, turning as needed, about 5 minutes. Remove the falafel with a slotted spoon and drain on paper towels. Season with salt.

Serve the falafel with the pea puree and charred corn, and garnish with the mâche and radish slices. Season with sea salt, dot with the pink chile mayo, and drizzle with olive oil.

BUTTERMILK POACHED LOBSTER WITH SWEET PEAS, RUTABAGA, AND MARIGOLD CURRY

SERVES 2

MARIGOLD CURRY

2 cups petals from unsprayed,
    organically grown marigolds
1 teaspoon ground fenugreek
½ teaspoon ground ginger
½ teaspoon ground cardamom
½ teaspoon ground turmeric
½ teaspoon ground fennel
½ teaspoon ground coriander

CHILE OIL

4 or 5 serrano chiles
1 cup extra-virgin olive oil
Kosher salt

1 cup fresh English peas
Kosher salt
1 (2½-pound) fresh lobster
2 cups buttermilk
2 cups heavy cream
1 medium rutabaga
Fresh pea tendrils, for garnish

Make the curry. Arrange the flower petals on a baking sheet and dry in a low (275°F) oven for 3 hours. (You can also use a dehydrator to dry the petals.) Reserve a few dehydrated leaves for garnish. Place the rest in a spice grinder with the fenugreek, ginger, cardamom, turmeric, fennel, and coriander, and grind the mixture to a fine powder.

Make the chile oil. Split the chiles open lengthwise and place in a small saucepan. Add the olive oil and season lightly with salt. Set over medium-low heat and slowly heat the oil for 15 to 20 minutes. Do not let the oil bubble. Once warmed through completely, remove from the heat and allow the chiles to cool completely in the oil. Strain the oil, discarding the chiles.

Cook the peas. Add the peas and ¼ cup of water to a small saucepan, season with salt, and set over high heat. Steam the peas 2 to 3 minutes, until tender. Set a few peas aside for garnish; puree the rest in a blender with a little of the steaming water until completely smooth.

Poach the lobster. Kill the lobster by inserting the tip of a sharp knife an inch or so behind the eyes and then cutting down toward the eyes. Separate the tail and claws from the body. Cut the tail into 4 sections, cutting between every second joint of the hard shell. Heat the buttermilk and cream in a saucepan. When the liquid starts to simmer, add the claws and tail pieces. Poach for 4 to 5 minutes, until the lobster shell is red and the flesh is just cooked. Remove and set aside to cool slightly, reserving the poaching liquid. Remove the flesh from the shells.

Prepare the rutabaga. Peel the rutabaga and slice very thinly on a mandoline. Bring a pot of salted water to a boil, and blanch the slices for 30 seconds, until translucent. Drain and keep warm.

Serve the lobster pieces with the pea puree, some of the buttermilk poaching liquid, and fresh pea tendrils. Top each piece of lobster with a thin slice of rutabaga. Garnish with some reserved peas and marigold petals. Drizzle with a little of the serrano chile oil. Dust with the marigold curry powder.

lobster

In early February 2012 Maine's lobster catch exceeded 100 million pounds for the first time in recorded history. With well-collaborated conservation efforts between lobstermen and local and federal wildlife management, lobster populations are at an all-time high. The boom in the industry has created a national lobster craze. As the price per pound has fallen, people are eating lobster again and for the first time. But now there seems to be too much of a good thing. The mild winter and warm spring that some scientists are pinning on global warming has caused lobsters to shed their shells early. As the lobster molts, what's left behind is known as a "soft-shell" lobster that hasn't fully developed its new rugged exoskeleton. Prized by locals, soft-shell lobsters are considered more succulent and have a sweeter flavor; the problem is that they don't travel well. "Shedders," as they are also called, have a mortality rate five times higher than hard-shell lobsters once they are taken out of the water and last for only a few days. The results are a glut in the market that has driven the "at boat" price down to $3.00 a pound, leaving lobstermen little choice but to self-impose a moratorium, leaving their boats tied to the docks. Hard-shell Maine lobsters that are shipped around the world are responsible for $313 million in the local economy and thousands of regional jobs. By eating a few more lobster rolls this year, you'll be providing much-needed balance in the market to get our guys back out on the water to make a decent living for their families as their fathers did before them.

RARE BEEF WITH HORSERADISH, RAISINS, CAPERS, AND CRISP YUKON CHIPS

SERVES 4

TENDERLOIN
¾ pound beef tenderloin, trimmed
Flaky sea salt and freshly cracked black pepper
Extra-virgin olive oil

HORSERADISH DRESSING
¼ cup grated fresh horseradish
½ cup sour cream
1 teaspoon honey
Juice of ½ lemon
1 tablespoon extra-virgin olive oil
Kosher salt and freshly cracked black pepper

2 tablespoons raisins
1 tablespoon honey

YUKON CHIPS
2 medium Yukon Gold potatoes
Canola oil, for deep frying
Kosher salt

3 tablespoons toasted pine nuts
2 tablespoons salt-packed capers, rinsed
    and drained
Radish sprouts

Make the tenderloin. Roll the beef tenderloin in a very light amount of salt and cracked black pepper. Set a large, heavy skillet over high heat. Add a drizzle of olive oil and sear the meat on all four sides until well browned, 5 to 6 minutes total. Take the meat out of the pan, wrap it tightly in plastic to form a nice even cylinder shape, and refrigerate until it gets cold, about 2 hours.

Make the horseradish dressing. Combine the grated horseradish, sour cream, honey, lemon juice, and olive oil in a bowl and whisk together. Season with salt and plenty of cracked black pepper.

Plump the raisins. Stir the raisins and honey together in a small bowl. Add hot water to cover, and rehydrate for 15 minutes. When the raisins are soft and plump, drain and pat dry on a paper towel.

Make the Yukon chips. Use a mandoline to finely slice the potatoes into chips. Place the chips in a bowl of ice water and rinse 2 or 3 times, until the water runs clear. Drain, and pat dry on paper towels. Heat 2 to 3 inches of canola oil to 350°F in a large, heavy pot. Add the chips in small batches and fry for 4 to 5 minutes, until golden and crispy. Drain on paper towels and season immediately with salt.

To serve, remove the beef from the fridge and, using a sharp knife, carefully cut it into very thin slices. Serve on top of the Yukon chips, scattered with the plumped raisins, toasted pine nuts, and capers. Drizzle with the horseradish dressing and garnish with radish sprouts.

CALIFORNIA GRASS-FED BEEF WITH SPINACH, PARMESAN, LEMON, AND OLIVE OIL

SERVES 2

1 head garlic
Extra-virgin olive oil

TUSCAN SPINACH

2 pounds spinach
2 tablespoons unsalted butter
2 tablespoons extra-virgin olive oil
2 garlic cloves, lightly smashed
1 cup heavy cream
¼ teaspoon freshly grated nutmeg
½ cup freshly grated Parmigiano-Reggiano
Kosher salt and freshly cracked black pepper

CHARRED LEMON

1 lemon, halved lengthwise

STEAK

Grapeseed oil
1 (1-pound) flatiron steak
Kosher salt and freshly cracked black pepper

½ cup shaved Parmigiano-Reggiano
Fresh baby spinach leaves

Roast the garlic. Preheat the oven to 350ºF. Break the garlic head into unpeeled cloves and place them on a sheet of foil. Drizzle with a little olive oil and then fold the foil to form a pouch and seal tightly. Roast in the oven for 20 to 25 minutes. When done, remove from the oven and open the pouch (so the garlic doesn't steam). Set aside until ready to serve.

Make the spinach. Wash the spinach in several changes of water to get rid of any grit. Drain the spinach, but keep some of the water clinging to the leaves. Heat the butter and olive oil in a large cast-iron skillet over medium-high heat, and add the spinach and garlic. Cook, turning frequently, until the spinach is wilted down evenly. Remove the garlic. Put the spinach into a colander and drain well, pressing out as much liquid as you can. Chop the spinach coarsely. Heat the same cast-iron skillet over medium-high heat, and add the cream and nutmeg; cook until it reduces by half, about 5 minutes. Add the spinach and Parmesan, and season with salt and pepper. Stir until the spinach is hot. Keep warm.

Char the lemon halves. Heat a grill to high. Grill the lemon halves cut-side down directly over high heat for about 2 minutes, until they are well marked.

Cook the steak. Preheat the oven to 375ºF. Set a large sauté pan over high heat, and when it is smoking hot, add a drizzle of grapeseed oil. Pat the steak dry with paper towels, then season it all over with salt and pepper. Sear the steak in the pan, 3 to 4 minutes per side, so it forms a nice crust with deep color. Transfer the steak to a plate, tent it with foil, and allow to rest for 5 to 6 minutes.

Cut the steak into thick slices and serve with the creamed spinach and roasted garlic cloves. Top with the shaved Parmesan and garnish with the charred lemon halves and some baby spinach leaves.

BABY BEETS, AVOCADO, GRAPEFRUIT, QUINOA, AND SORREL

SERVES 4

BEETS

2 bunches assorted baby beets (such as red, golden, Chioggia)
2 tablespoons extra-virgin olive oil
Kosher salt and freshly cracked black pepper

RED QUINOA

1½ cups red quinoa
Kosher salt
1 teaspoon fresh lemon juice

CRUSHED AVOCADO

2 ripe avocados
1 tablespoon extra-virgin olive oil
¼ teaspoon fresh lemon juice
Kosher salt

GRAPEFRUIT VINAIGRETTE

½ cup ruby red grapefruit juice
½ teaspoon grated grapefruit zest
1 tablespoon light agave syrup
¼ teaspoon whole-grain mustard
3 tablespoons plain yogurt
¼ cup grapeseed oil
Pinch kosher salt

1 ruby grapefruit
1 bunch fresh sorrel leaves
½ avocado, sliced
1 tablespoon tender beet greens

Wash and lightly scrub the beets and pat them dry. Select 3 beets, preferably 1 of each color, for garnish. Slice them finely on a mandoline or with a sharp knife. Place in a bowl of ice water and set aside until ready to use.

Cook the beets. Preheat the oven to 350°F. Place the remaining beets on a large sheet of foil. Drizzle with the olive oil and season with salt and pepper. Bring the edges of the foil together and fold to form a packet, poking a few holes in the top to allow steam to escape. Place on a baking sheet and bake in the oven for 1 hour. When done, the tip of a paring knife should be able to pierce the beet with little resistance. Remove and discard the beet skins. Quarter the beets and pour the juices and oil from the pouch over the beets to keep them moist.

Make the red quinoa. In a medium saucepan, bring 3 cups of water to a boil over high heat. Add the quinoa, then reduce the heat and simmer uncovered for 10 to 12 minutes, until tender. Season with salt and the lemon juice, and stir well. Spread on a plate to cool and set aside.

Prepare the avocado. Halve and pit the avocados. Scoop out the flesh with a tablespoon and place in a mixing bowl. Mash the avocados and olive oil with a fork, leaving them somewhat chunky. Season with the lemon juice and salt.

Make the vinaigrette. Combine all the vinaigrette ingredients in a blender and puree until slightly emulsified.

Use a sharp knife to slice off the rind and pith from the grapefruit. Cut between the membranes to free the grapefruit segments.

To assemble, arrange sorrel leaves on each plate. Top with some cooled quinoa, roasted beets, sliced avocado, and a quenelle of crushed avocado. Garnish with the grapefruit segments, beet greens, beet slices, and vinaigrette.

beets

Known as the bloody heart of the vegetable world, beets are a natural, vitamin-rich source of iron. According to the Centers for Disease Control, iron deficiency is the most common nutritional deficiency worldwide. It can cause mild to severe cases of anemia, a condition in which the body does not have enough healthy red blood cells to carry oxygen to the body's tissues. The lack of efficient blood flow and low levels of oxygen in the blood can wear you down, leaving you feeling constantly exhausted. Other symptoms of iron-deficient anemia include shortness of breath, rapid heartbeat, chronic headache, dizziness, and loss of sex drive. The nitric acid that beets produce in your body opens up blood vessels so that blood can surge through your body. The hyperalert sensation that you feel after drinking beet juice is a rush of oxygen going to your brain. Adding beets to your diet can be as easy as drinking beet juice instead of an afternoon coffee or buying roasted beets from your neighborhood deli. A study in 2009 by the *Journal of Applied Physiology* found that athletes who consumed 16 ounces of beet juice on six consecutive days were able to sustain low-intensity activities with less effort and were able to achieve a 16 percent improvement in high-intensity performance. The study goes on to say that "improvements seen in the subjects drinking beet juice have not been achieved by any other known means, including long-term endurance exercise training."

BEET TARTARE, TEMPURA ONION PETALS, HORSERADISH AIOLI, AND CHERVIL

SERVES 4

BEET TARTARE
3 medium red beets
2 tablespoons extra-virgin olive oil
Kosher salt and freshly cracked black pepper

HORSERADISH AIOLI
1 egg white
1 ½ tablespoons prepared horseradish
1 ½ teaspoons fresh lemon juice
1 ½ cups grapeseed oil
Kosher salt

TEMPURA BATTER
1 ½ cups all-purpose flour, plus extra for dredging
½ cup cornstarch
1 ½ teaspoons salt
1 ½ cups ice-cold club soda

ONION PETALS
Canola oil, for deep frying
2 large Vidalia onions
All-purpose flour
Kosher salt

Chopped fresh chives
Fresh chervil leaves
2 ounces salmon roe
Flaky sea salt

Roast the beets. Preheat the oven to 350°F. Wash and lightly scrub the beets. Pat them dry and place on a sheet of foil. Drizzle with 1 tablespoon of the olive oil and season well with salt and pepper. Wrap the foil tightly to form a packet, poking a few holes to allow steam to escape, and place on a baking sheet. Roast for 1 hour, or until the beets are tender. Remove from the oven, and while still warm, carefully peel off and discard the skins. Place the beets in a food processor and add a little of the roasting liquid from the packet. Pulse 10 to 12 times, until the beets are finely chopped but still have some texture. Season with a drizzle of the remaining 1 tablespoon olive oil and with salt and pepper. Set aside.

Make the horseradish aioli. In a blender, combine the egg white, horseradish, and lemon juice. Blend until creamy. Then, with the blender running, slowly drizzle in the grapeseed oil until the mixture emulsifies. Season with salt. Refrigerate until ready to use.

Make the tempura batter. In a large mixing bowl, combine the flour, cornstarch, and salt. Make a well in the center and gradually pour in the club soda, whisking constantly and working your way from the center out to slowly incorporate the dry ingredients and form a smooth batter.

Fry the onion petals. Heat 3 to 4 inches of canola oil to 375°F in a large pot. Peel the onions and cut each into 6 wedges. Separate the layers and discard the smaller inner layers. Working in small batches, dredge the "petals" in flour and then lightly coat in the tempura batter. Fry until crisp and golden, 4 to 5 minutes. Remove from the oil, drain on paper towels, and season with salt.

To assemble, place the onion petals on a large platter cupped-side up. Serve with spoonfuls of the beet tartare and dot with the horseradish aioli. Garnish with the chopped chives, chervil leaves, and salmon roe. Season with flaky sea salt.

PICKLED BEETS WITH SALMON, SPROUTS, AND FROMAGE BLANC

SERVES 4 TO 6

PICKLED BEETS
4 medium red beets
2 cups white vinegar
1 cup sugar
½ teaspoon caraway seeds
1 teaspoon kosher salt
½ small onion, finely sliced

SALMON
1 whole side of boneless, skin-on salmon
    (about 1½ pounds)
Kosher salt
Extra-virgin olive oil

1 ruby grapefruit
½ pound fromage blanc
1 teaspoon fresh lemon juice
¼ cup white daikon radish sprouts
Extra-virgin olive oil
Flaky sea salt

Pickle the beets. Scrub the beets, then slice them into ¼-inch-thick disks. In a medium pot, combine the vinegar, sugar, caraway seeds, and salt. Bring to a boil, then reduce to a simmer. Add the beets and the onion slices. Simmer for 25 to 30 minutes, until tender. Remove from the heat and allow the beets to cool in the pickling mixture.

Prepare the salmon. Preheat the oven to 300°F. Using a very sharp filleting knife, carefully remove the skin from the fish fillet in one piece, reserving the skin. Thinly slice the salmon flesh, and refrigerate until ready to serve. Line a baking sheet with parchment or a silicone mat. Place the skin in the center of the parchment and spread it completely flat. Season it with a little salt and drizzle with a little olive oil. Place another sheet of parchment on top of the skin, then place a second baking sheet on top to hold the skin flat. Place the baking sheets in the oven and bake the salmon skin for 25 minutes, until completely crispy and golden. Place the crispy skin on a wire rack and allow to cool completely.

Use a sharp knife to slice off the rind and pith from the grapefruit. Cut between the membranes to free the grapefruit segments. Whip the fromage blanc with the lemon juice until light and creamy. Transfer the beet slices to a serving plate, draining off any excess liquid. Top with the salmon slices and grapefruit segments, and dot with the fromage blanc. Garnish with the sprouts and a few pieces of pickled onion. Drizzle with a little olive oil and season with sea salt. Dress very lightly with some pickling liquid from the beets. Break the crispy salmon skin into small pieces and scatter over the top.

FRISÉE SALAD WITH BLUEBERRIES, CANDIED PECANS, WHIPPED BLUE CHEESE, AND BUTTERMILK DRESSING

SERVES 4

CANDIED PECANS
1½ cups pecan halves
1 teaspoon vegetable oil
½ cup sugar
½ teaspoon flaky sea salt

BUTTERMILK DRESSING
⅓ cup buttermilk
¼ cup sour cream
¼ cup mayonnaise
2 tablespoons extra-virgin olive oil
2 tablespoons fresh lemon juice
Pinch grated lemon zest
1 teaspoon fresh tarragon leaves
Kosher salt and freshly cracked black pepper

1 pint fresh blueberries
1 tablespoon sugar
Juice of ½ lemon
Extra-virgin olive oil
½ cup crème fraîche, at room temperature
1½ cups crumbled mild blue cheese,
    such as Humboldt Fog
1 large head frisée lettuce
2 tablespoons fresh tarragon leaves

Make the pecans. Preheat the oven to 350°F. Place the pecans on a baking sheet, drizzle with the vegetable oil, and toss to coat evenly. Toast in the oven for 15 to 20 minutes, until browned. Make the caramel by combining the sugar and 2 tablespoons of water in a saucepan and simmering over medium heat until the sugar is completely dissolved. Cook for 7 to 10 minutes, watching carefully until it turns amber. Add the salt and remove from the heat. Fold in the pecans and stir to coat evenly. Turn out onto waxed paper and use a fork to separate the pecans so they don't stick together as they cool.

Make the buttermilk dressing. Combine all the dressing ingredients in a blender and puree until smooth. Refrigerate until ready to use.

Put ¼ cup of the blueberries in a saucepan and add ¼ cup of water, the sugar, and the lemon juice. Heat gently over low heat until the blueberries just start to bleed. Remove from the heat, add a drizzle of olive oil, and stir.

Combine the crème fraîche and crumbled blue cheese in a large bowl. Using a whisk, stir vigorously until well combined. Set aside.

Wash the lettuce and discard the dark green outer leaves as these are bitter. Remove the core and tear the lettuce into bite-size pieces. Smear a little of the dressing on each plate and arrange the lettuce and raw blueberries on top. Scatter with candied pecans, garnish with tarragon leaves, and top with scoops of whipped blue cheese. Dot the plates with the liquid from the cooked blueberries.

STRAWBERRIES WITH PARMESAN, BASIL, AND BALSAMIC

SERVES 2 TO 4

BALSAMIC PEARLS

3 to 4 cups olive oil
1.5 grams agar agar powder
100 grams balsamic vinegar

STRAWBERRY CHIPS

4 to 6 large fresh strawberries
2 tablespoons confectioners' sugar

1 pound fresh strawberries
¼ cup Parmigiano-Reggiano shavings
2 tablespoons flowering basil
1 tablespoon micro sprouts
Extra-virgin olive oil

Prepare the balsamic pearls. Pour the olive oil into a tall, clear vessel, like a large beer glass, and place it in the freezer to chill to about 38°F, about 30 minutes.

Combine the agar agar and balsamic in a small saucepan and bring to a boil. Stir to completely dissolve the agar agar. Let cool for 5 minutes, to about 125°F. Then transfer the mixture to a large plastic syringe or a squeeze bottle. Carefully dispense drops into the olive oil to form "pearls," allowing them to sink to the bottom. Drain the pearls when ready to use, reserving the olive oil for another use.

Make the strawberry chips. Preheat the oven to 300°F. Thinly slice the strawberries lengthwise. Line a baking sheet with parchment or a silicone mat, and arrange the slices evenly on the sheet. Sprinkle with the confectioners' sugar. Bake for 2 hours, or until the strawberries are dehydrated and crisp.

To assemble, halve the fresh strawberries lengthwise. Top with the balsamic pearls, Parmesan shavings, basil flowers, and sprouts. Garnish with the dried strawberry chips. Dot with a little extra-virgin olive oil.

making "pearls"

Perhaps more than any other technique, spherification has come to symbolize the culinary flourishes of molecular gastronomy. Originally discovered by Unilever in the 1950s, the technique was made famous by Ferran Adrià at elBulli in Roses, Spain. When a base liquid is mixed with sodium alginate, then dipped into a cold solution of calcium chloride, a sphere of liquid held by a thin gel membrane is produced.

My hybrid technique is actually easy to pull off at home and uses fewer ingredients. It works with just about any liquid, from consommés to fruit juices. I've substituted organic agar agar, an extract of seaweed, for the chemicals necessary to produce gel-encapsulated spheres. It's not exactly the same thing, but it's still delicious, with a toothsome chew rather than a liquid pop—similar to a gummy bear, but natural. The method is simple; the trick is being precise at each step.

To create balsamic pearls, boil the vinegar with the agar agar powder, then cool to 125°F. In a narrow container that's at least 12 inches tall, chill the olive oil to 38°F. Using a squeeze bottle or plastic syringe, dispense the agar agar liquid into the near-freezing olive oil one drop at a time. If the container is too short or the oil isn't cold enough, the pearls won't set in time or be firm enough and they will "pancake" when they hit the bottom of the glass. Conversely, if the oil is too cold, the pearls will set instantly upon contact, making weird tadpole shapes. Stored in the olive oil, the pearls can last for months in the refrigerator.

STRAWBERRY ALMOND MESS

SERVES 4 TO 6

WHIPPED HONEY CREAM
1 pint heavy cream
½ cup orange blossom honey
2 egg yolks

LAVENDER HONEY
¼ cup orange blossom honey
2-inch strip orange peel
4 to 5 fresh lavender stems

TUILE COOKIES
3 large egg whites
¼ teaspoon kosher salt
½ cup confectioners' sugar
¼ teaspoon almond extract
½ cup all-purpose flour
4 tablespoons (½ stick) unsalted butter, melted
¼ cup crushed toasted almonds

2 pints ripe California strawberries
Edible flower petals
Fresh strawberry blossoms

Prepare the whipped honey cream. In a bowl, whip the cream, honey, and egg yolks together until soft peaks form. Keep chilled until ready to serve.

Prepare the lavender honey. Combine the honey, orange peel, lavender stems, and 2 tablespoons of water in a small saucepan. Set over low heat and warm for 15 to 20 minutes to slowly infuse the honey mixture with lavender and orange. Then strain the honey and set aside.

Make the tuile cookies. Preheat the oven to 350°F and line a half sheet pan with a silicone baking mat. In the bowl of an electric mixer fitted with the whisk attachment, whip the egg whites and salt until just foamy. Reduce the speed to medium, and add the confectioners' sugar and almond extract. Gradually sprinkle in the flour and continue to mix until completely incorporated. Increase the speed to medium and pour in the melted butter. Whisk until well combined and slightly thickened.

Baking the cookies in batches, drop level tablespoons of the batter onto the lined baking sheet, spacing them about 6 inches apart. Using a wet offset spatula, spread the batter into 4-inch rounds. (You can also use a flat round stencil to make precise shapes if desired.) Sprinkle the tops with some crushed almonds, and then bake in the middle of the oven until the cookies turn an even golden brown, exactly 7 minutes. Remove from the oven and carefully transfer to a wire rack to cool.

Place the strawberries in individual bowls. Break the tuile cookies into bite-size pieces and sprinkle them over the strawberries. Top with spoonfuls of whipped honey cream and garnish with flower petals and strawberry blossoms. Drizzle with the lavender honey, and serve.

strawberries

Doing something as simple as eating strawberries on a daily basis can have a major impact on how your body defends itself and neutralizes inflammation. The phytonutrients in strawberries are a powerful antioxidant, third behind blackberries and walnuts in nutrient absorption, and strawberries contain more vitamin C than oranges.

Managing cancer risk has a lot to do with managing inflammation. If you've ever cut your finger or jammed your toe you've seen inflammation in action. The redness and swelling are the body's defense mechanisms as it begins the repair process. Not all inflammation is as obvious as that. Aging is a domino effect that can take years to recognize. Inflammation at the cellular level can silently, over time, negatively affect your health. A poor diet of refined sugars and environmental toxins like cigarettes can escalate the domino effect that leads to cell damage. Dead or dying cells that can't heal themselves promote an environment that fosters genomic lesions and tumor initiation. Every modern disease is either caused or affected by inflammation. Taking an offensive position with the quality of food you put in your body gives your cells a much stronger defense against cell mutation.

BUTTERMILK PANNA COTTA, CHERRIES, PISTACHIOS, AND BASIL

SERVES 8

PANNA COTTA
1 envelope (¼ ounce) powdered gelatin
2 cups buttermilk
1 cup heavy cream
¾ cup superfine sugar
½ teaspoon grated lemon zest
2 vanilla beans, split and scraped

Nonstick cooking spray

POACHED CHERRIES
2 cups California pinot noir
1¼ cups sugar
1 vanilla bean, split and scraped
1 cinnamon stick
4 whole cloves
3-inch strip orange peel
1 pound fresh cherries, pitted

½ cup tapioca
¼ cup shelled unsalted pistachios
2 tablespoons rock salt
Fresh basil buds
Extra-virgin olive oil

Prepare the panna cotta. Put the gelatin in a small bowl and add ½ cup of the buttermilk. Whisk to combine and set aside. In a medium pot, combine the remaining 1½ cups buttermilk with the cream, sugar, lemon zest, and vanilla beans (both seeds and pods). Set over high heat and bring to a boil. Then reduce the heat and simmer for 5 minutes. Add the gelatin mixture and whisk well. Pass through a strainer into a bowl to remove any lumps, and discard the vanilla pods. Spray 8 small ramekins lightly with nonstick cooking spray, and divide the panna cotta evenly among them. Chill in the fridge for 3 to 4 hours, until set.

Poach the cherries. In a medium saucepan, combine the wine, sugar, vanilla bean (both seeds and pod), cinnamon stick, cloves, and orange peel. Bring to a simmer over high heat, then add the cherries. Reduce the heat and simmer, partially covered, until the cherries are plump and tender, about 7 minutes. Remove from the heat and strain, reserving the liquid. Set the cherries aside and discard the cinnamon, cloves, vanilla pod, and orange peel. Return the poaching liquid to the saucepan and set aside.

Prepare the tapioca pearls. Soak the tapioca pearls in cold water to cover for 45 minutes. Then drain and add them to the reserved cherry poaching liquid in the saucepan. Set over high heat and bring to a boil. Reduce the heat to a bare simmer and gently cook the tapioca for 30 minutes. Remove from the heat and allow the tapioca to steep in the red wine mixture. Strain before serving, reserving the liquid.

Crush the pistachios. Combine the pistachios and rock salt in a mortar and gently crush together with a pestle.

To assemble, carefully unmold the panna cottas onto individual plates. Top each one with some poached cherries, some of the tapioca pearls, and some of the cherry poaching liquid. Garnish with crushed salted pistachios, basil buds, and a few drops of extra-virgin olive oil.

BUTTERNUT SQUASH
TORTELLINI WITH LENTILS, YOGURT, AND SUMAC

SERVES 4 TO 6

SQUASH
1 medium butternut squash
Extra-virgin olive oil
Kosher salt and freshly cracked black pepper

PASTA
1½ cups all-purpose flour, plus extra for dusting
1 egg plus 1 yolk, lightly beaten
1 tablespoon olive oil
1 egg, beaten, for egg wash

LENTILS
2 cups lentilles du Puy (French lentils)
2 lemon slices
1 small onion, quartered
2 tablespoons curry powder
Kosher salt and freshly cracked black pepper
¼ cup extra-virgin olive oil

SAUCE
2 tablespoons unsalted butter
2 tablespoons extra-virgin olive oil
Kosher salt

¼ cup chopped roasted Jimmy Nardello peppers, crushed to a pulp with a mortar and pestle and a little olive oil
1½ cups plain Greek yogurt
Fresh thyme buds
Ground sumac

Roast the squash. Preheat the oven to 350°F. Peel the squash and cut it in half lengthwise. Scoop out the seeds, then cut the flesh into large chunks. Place on a baking sheet, drizzle with olive oil, and season with salt and pepper. Roast for 35 to 40 minutes, until very tender. Transfer the roasted squash to a large bowl, season once more, and add more olive oil. Using a potato masher, mash until you have a chunky puree. Set aside to cool.

Make the pasta dough. Mound the flour on a clean work surface. Make a well in the center and add the beaten egg and yolk and the olive oil. Stir the liquids together. Then, using a fork, slowly incorporate a little flour at a time, working from the walls of the well out. Once everything has been incorporated, use your hands to knead the dough and work it into a smooth ball. Add a little water as required if the dough is too dry. Form the dough into a disk, then wrap it tightly in plastic and refrigerate for 30 minutes to rest.

Make the lentils. Place the lentils in a large pot. Add water to cover by 2 inches and the lemon, onion, curry powder, and salt. Bring to a boil, then simmer for 25 to 30 minutes, until tender. Drain the lentils, discarding the onion and lemon. Season with salt and pepper, and add the olive oil.

Form the tortellini. Divide the dough into 4 portions and roll out using either a machine or a rolling pin about 1/16 inch thick. Cut into 2½-inch squares and cover with a damp towel. Place ½ teaspoon of the squash in the middle of a pasta square. Use a pastry brush to wet the edges with egg wash, then fold over to make a triangle and press together firmly to seal. Bring the two points at the base of the triangle together and use egg wash to seal them. Set the formed pasta on a lightly floured baking sheet so they don't stick together. Reserve the remaining mashed squash.

Make the sauce. In a small sauté pan, cook the butter over medium heat for about 2 minutes, until the milk solids are golden and the butter smells nutty. Pour into a large mixing bowl and add the olive oil. Season with salt. Keep warm.

Set a large pot of salted water over high heat and bring to a boil. Cook the pasta, in batches, in the boiling water until they float to the surface, 2 to 3 minutes. Use a strainer to remove the pasta from the water and add them to the bowl with the sauce. Add a bit of the pasta cooking water, up to 1/3 cup, and swirl to coat the pasta. Season with salt.

Serve the stuffed pasta on a bed of lentils. Top with additional squash puree, crushed peppers, and a spoonful of Greek yogurt. Spoon the browned butter sauce over all, and garnish with thyme buds and ground sumac.

ROASTED BUTTERNUT SQUASH ARANCINI, FRIED DUCK EGG, SAUSAGE GRAVY, AND SAGE

SERVES 6

SQUASH

3 cups ½-inch cubes of butternut squash
    (about ½ squash)
Extra-virgin olive oil
Kosher salt and freshly cracked black pepper
1 teaspoon fresh lemon juice

ARANCINI

Extra-virgin olive oil, for shallow frying
¼ cup diced shallots
2 cups Arborio rice
1 cup dry white wine
Kosher salt and freshly cracked black pepper
½ cup (1 stick) unsalted butter
½ cup grated Parmigiano-Reggiano
Canola oil, for deep frying

SAUSAGE GRAVY

¼ cup extra-virgin olive oil
24 fresh sage leaves
1 pound loose sweet fennel sausage
3 tablespoons all-purpose flour
2 cups whole milk
Plenty of freshly cracked black pepper
Kosher salt

2 tablespoons extra-virgin olive oil
6 fresh duck eggs
Kosher salt and freshly cracked black pepper

Roast the squash. Preheat the oven to 350°F. Spread the squash pieces on a baking sheet in a single layer. Drizzle with olive oil, season with salt and pepper, and roast for 25 to 30 minutes, until tender. Transfer to a food processor and add the lemon juice and 3 or 4 tablespoons of water; puree until smooth.

Prepare the arancini mixture. Make a risotto: Place a large pot over medium heat and add an inch of olive oil. Add the shallots and cook for 5 minutes, until soft and translucent. Stir in the rice, making sure to coat all the grains with the oil. Add the wine and cook until most of the liquid has evaporated. Ladle in 1 cup of hot water. Using a wooden spoon, stir gently until most of the water has been absorbed. Continue to add hot water, 1 cup at a time, stirring until each addition has been absorbed. After 15 to 20 minutes, test the rice. It should be cooked and creamy but still have a slight bite to it. Season with salt and pepper; stir in the butter and Parmesan. Set aside ½ cup of the squash puree, and fold the rest into the risotto. Give it a final taste for seasoning. Spread the risotto out on a baking sheet and cool in the refrigerator for 30 minutes.

Make the sausage gravy. Heat a large cast-iron skillet over medium-high heat. Add the olive oil and sage leaves. As the oil heats, the sage will crackle and infuse the oil. When the leaves are cooked and translucent but still green, remove them from the pan and set aside to drain on paper towels; reserve for garnish. Add the sausage to the pan and cook for 8 to 10 minutes, until well browned and cooked through, breaking it up with a wooden spoon as it cooks. Use a slotted spoon to transfer the sausage to a bowl, leaving the rendered fat in the skillet. Whisk the flour into the fat and cook, stirring continuously, for 2 to 3 minutes to make a roux. Whisk the milk into the skillet and bring the gravy to a boil. Lower the heat and simmer gently for 2 minutes. Stir in the sausage, and season with plenty of freshly cracked black pepper and some salt. Keep warm.

Form and cook the arancini. Fill a large pot with 3 inches of canola oil and heat it to 350°F. Roll the risotto into small bite-size balls, and then flatten them into gnocchi-size cylinders. Working in batches, fry the arancini in the hot oil for 3 to 4 minutes, until golden and lightly crispy. Drain on paper towels and season immediately with salt.

Fry the duck eggs. Set a large nonstick sauté pan over high heat. Add the olive oil and when it is lightly smoking, crack the duck eggs into the pan one at a time. Cook the eggs sunny-side up for 3 to 4 minutes so the yolks are still runny. Season with salt.

Serve the crispy fried duck eggs with the sausage gravy, reserved squash puree, and arancini. Garnish with the crispy sage leaves and a few turns of cracked black pepper.

WHOLE WHEAT PASTA, BUTTERNUT SQUASH PUREE, BLACK TRUFFLE, AND SAGE

SERVES 4

SQUASH
2 medium butternut squash (about 3 pounds total)
1 tablespoon extra-virgin olive oil
Kosher salt and freshly cracked black pepper

Olive oil, for shallow frying
16 fresh sage leaves
1 medium onion, sliced
Kosher salt and freshly cracked black pepper
Juice of 1 lemon
1 tablespoon black truffle oil
1 pound fresh whole wheat spaghetti
½ cup shaved Parmigiano-Reggiano
2 to 3 ounces fresh black truffle, finely shaved
Fleur de sel and freshly cracked black pepper
Black truffle oil

Cook the squash. Preheat the oven to 350°F and line a baking sheet with parchment or a silicone mat. Peel the butternut squash and trim off the top cylinder of one. Using a mandoline or a sharp knife, finely slice the cylinder into chips and arrange them in a single layer on the prepared baking sheet. Drizzle with the olive oil and season with salt and pepper. Bake for 20 minutes, until crisp. Set aside. Halve the remaining squash and discard the seeds. Cut the squash into bite-size pieces.

In a large sauté pan, heat ½ inch of olive oil over medium-high heat. Add the sage leaves and fry until crisp, 30 to 40 seconds. Drain on paper towels and set aside. Add the onion and reserved uncooked squash to the pan and sauté for 7 to 8 minutes, until the vegetables are caramelized and starting to become tender. Season with salt and pepper. Add 2 cups of water and bring to a simmer. Cook for 5 to 7 minutes, until the squash is tender. Transfer to a food processor, add the lemon juice and truffle oil, and puree until smooth. Season once more with salt and pepper. Set aside and keep warm.

Cook the pasta. Bring a large pot of salted water to a rolling boil. Add the pasta and cook for 4 to 5 minutes, until just al dente. Drain the pasta and return it to the pot. Fold in the butternut squash puree, tossing to coat everything evenly.

To serve, use a carving fork to lift up the pasta and twirl it around the tines. Set the pasta out neatly on each plate and top with the butternut squash chips, fried sage leaves, shaved Parmesan, and shaved black truffle. Finish with fleur de sel, cracked black pepper, and a drizzle of truffle oil.

truffles

Truffles hit the button as the most primal aroma on the planet—they were once described to me as a cross between socks and sex. While Piemonte gets most of the press for the *Tuber magnatum,* the large white truffle, my absolute favorites are the large black truffles harvested throughout Europe in the summer. Summer truffles from both Umbria and Burgundy can, in a good season, be prolific. And while they are still expensive, the more abundant black summer truffles can cost hundreds of dollars less per pound than Piemontese black truffles from the short early winter season or white truffles, which in some years can match the price of gold. The best way to truly taste the complexity of a truffle is to shave a few paper-thin slices onto the palm of your hand, add a few grains of good sea salt, wait thirty seconds to let your body temperature warm the oils of the truffle, then pop them in your mouth. A transcendent experience.

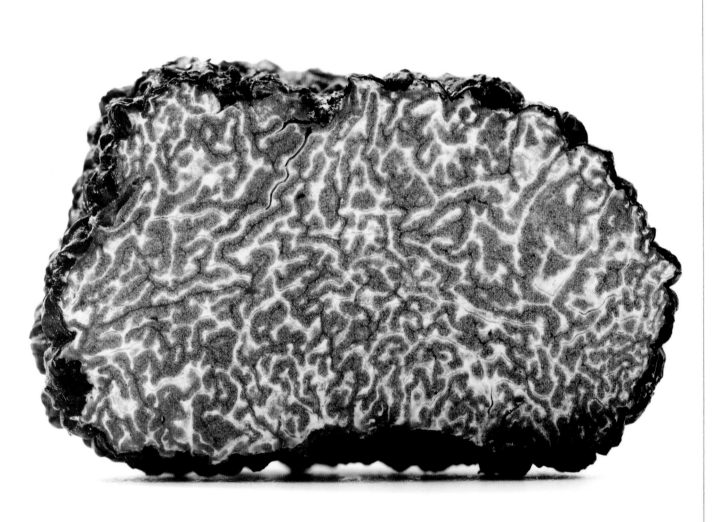

BUTTERNUT SQUASH PUREE WITH PAN-ROASTED PORCINIS AND BROWN BUTTER WITH SAGE

SERVES 4

BUTTERNUT SQUASH PUREE
1 large butternut squash
    (about 6 cups cubed flesh)
Extra-virgin olive oil
Kosher salt and freshly cracked black pepper
1 teaspoon fresh lemon juice
2 teaspoons sugar

PORCINIS
1½ pounds fresh porcini mushrooms
¼ cup extra-virgin olive oil
Kosher salt and freshly cracked black pepper
2 or 3 sprigs fresh thyme
2 tablespoons unsalted butter

SAGE BROWN BUTTER
¾ cup (1½ sticks) unsalted butter
6 to 8 fresh sage leaves
½ cup pecan halves
Kosher salt
¼ cup full-bodied red wine
1 teaspoon sugar

Make the squash puree. Preheat the oven to 350°F. Peel and halve the squash and discard the seeds. Cut into 1-inch cubes. Spread the squash pieces in a single layer on a roasting tray. Drizzle with olive oil, season with salt and pepper, and roast in the oven for 25 to 30 minutes, until tender. Transfer to a blender and puree with the lemon juice, sugar, and ½ cup of warm water until completely smooth.

Make the porcinis. Preheat the oven to 400°F. Clean the porcinis and cut them lengthwise into halves or quarters to make equal-size pieces. Set a large ovenproof sauté pan over high heat. Add the olive oil, and when nearly smoking, add the mushrooms but do not stir so they settle and get some good color on them. After 30 to 40 seconds, season with salt and pepper, then add the thyme and butter to the pan. Toss to coat everything evenly, place the pan in the oven, and roast for 10 to 12 minutes, until the mushrooms are well caramelized all over. Transfer to a bowl and set aside.

Make the brown butter. Wipe out the pan used to cook the mushrooms, then add the butter and melt over high heat. Once the butter is bubbly, add the sage leaves (take care, as they will crackle) and cook just until crisp. Remove from the pan with a slotted spoon and set aside. Add the pecans to the pan and cook for 2 to 3 minutes, until browned. Use a slotted spoon to transfer the pecans to a paper towel–lined plate to drain. Season both the crispy sage and the pecans with salt. Reduce the heat and continue to cook the butter until it is brown and solids have formed in the bottom of the pan, 5 to 6 minutes—it should be aromatic at this stage. Remove from the heat and whisk in the red wine and sugar. Continue to whisk to make a "vinaigrette."

Serve the roasted porcinis with the squash puree and dress generously with the brown butter vinaigrette. Garnish with the crispy sage and toasted pecans.

PUMPKIN PIE, WHIPPED EGGNOG, SAGE, AND HONEY

SERVES 6 TO 8

PUMPKIN

1 large sugar pumpkin
¼ cup orange blossom honey
3 tablespoons unsalted butter
½ teaspoon kosher salt
Canola oil, for deep-frying
1½ teaspoons ground cinnamon
⅓ cup sugar

PIE CRUST

2 cups all-purpose flour
5 teaspoons sugar
Pinch kosher salt
12 tablespoons (1½ sticks) cold unsalted butter,
   cut into pieces
3 tablespoons ice water, plus more if needed

EGGNOG

4 egg yolks
⅓ cup sugar
3 tablespoons brandy
¼ teaspoon ground cinnamon
⅛ teaspoon ground cloves
⅛ teaspoon ground nutmeg
1 pint heavy cream

2 tablespoons unsalted butter
10 to 12 fresh sage leaves
¼ cup honey

Bake the pumpkin. Preheat the oven to 350°F. Quarter the pumpkin and remove the seeds with a large spoon, keeping the fibers intact. Place the quarters cut-side up on a sheet tray. Place clusters of the pumpkin seeds on a second tray. Place both trays in the oven to roast: pumpkin seeds for 30 minutes and pumpkin pieces for 45 minutes.

Prepare the pie crust. Combine the flour, sugar, and salt in a large bowl. Mix in the cold butter with a pastry blender until the mixture resembles coarse bread crumbs. Add the ice water until the dough holds together. If it's still crumbly, add more ice water, 1 teaspoon at a time. Wrap in plastic wrap, and refrigerate for at least 30 minutes.

On a floured surface and using a floured rolling pin, roll out the dough to form an 11- to 12-inch round. Ease the dough into a 10-inch pie pan and press it firmly into the bottom and sides. Trim the excess dough. Use a fork to poke holes in the bottom of the crust. Chill for 15 minutes.

Increase the oven temperature to 375°F. Place a large piece of parchment paper on top of the dough and fill it with pie weights. Bake the crust for 10 minutes, then remove the parchment and weights and continue baking until the crust is golden, approximately 10 minutes longer. Cool completely.

Make the filling. Remove the skins from the roasted pumpkin pieces and place the pulp in a food processor. Add the honey, butter, and salt, and puree until completely smooth. Set aside and keep warm.

Fry the pumpkin seeds. Heat 2 to 3 inches of oil in a medium saucepan to 350°F. Add the pumpkin seed clusters and deep-fry for 2 to 3 minutes, until golden and crispy. Mix the cinnamon and sugar in a large bowl. Toss hot clusters of pumpkin seeds in the cinnamon sugar to coat evenly. Set aside.

Prepare the eggnog. Combine the egg yolks and sugar in a stand mixer fitted with the whisk attachment. Whip on high speed until the mixture becomes pale yellow and creamy. With the mixer running on medium speed, add the brandy and spices. Continue to mix until the ingredients are fully combined. In a separate bowl, whip the cream until just lightly thickened. Fold the thickened cream into the eggnog, and whip until the eggnog is light and creamy.

Heat the butter and sage leaves together in a small sauté pan over medium-high heat. As the butter heats up, the sage leaves will begin to cook and become translucent. Drain the sage leaves on paper towels. Add the honey to the butter remaining in the pan and stir until warmed through.

Just before serving, break the cooled pie crust into large pieces and place some on each plate. Smear warm pumpkin puree over the pieces of pie crust. Top with a spoonful of whipped eggnog, a scattering of pumpkin seeds, and a few fried sage leaves. Drizzle with the honey butter sauce.

HAWAIIAN TUNA WITH CONFIT CARROTS, SOY CARAMEL, AND CRISPY GINGER

SERVES 4

CONFIT CARROTS
1 pound organic carrots
1 tablespoon yellow mustard seeds
2 (1-inch) pieces fresh ginger
1 teaspoon low-sodium soy sauce
2 cups grapeseed oil, or more as needed

TUNA
1½ pounds sushi-grade center-cut ahi tuna
Extra-virgin olive oil
Kosher salt

SOY CARAMEL
½ cup sugar
¼ cup low-sodium soy sauce

Juice of 1 lemon

CRISPY GINGER
Canola oil, for shallow frying
1 large (2-inch) piece fresh ginger, unpeeled

Radish sprouts

Make the carrots. Preheat the oven to 300°F. Place the carrots in a baking dish that's just large enough to hold them and add the mustard seeds, ginger, and soy sauce. Add grapeseed oil to just cover the carrots, then cover the dish tightly with foil. Oven-braise the carrots for 1½ hours, until very tender. Allow the carrots to cool in the oil. Drain, reserving ½ cup of the braising oil, and slice the carrots into ½-inch-thick rounds. Set the reserved oil and sliced carrots aside separately, discarding the remaining braising oil or saving it for another use.

Sear the tuna. Cut the tuna into long rectangles 1 inch x 1 inch thick. Rub lightly with olive oil and season with salt. Heat a nonstick sauté pan or a cast-iron griddle over very high heat. Sear the tuna briefly on all four sides until just lightly colored (you want to keep the middle very rare). Transfer to a plate and chill for at least 30 minutes.

Make the soy caramel. Combine the sugar and ¼ cup of water in a small saucepan. Bring to a boil over high heat and simmer, swirling the mixture occasionally (do not stir it), until the mixture turns amber, 4 to 5 minutes. Immediately remove from the heat and stir in ¼ cup of the soy sauce. Set the saucepan into a bowl of ice water to quickly bring the soy caramel to room temperature.

In a small bowl, stir together 2 tablespoons of the soy caramel and 6 tablespoons of the reserved confit carrot oil. Add a good squeeze of lemon juice and whisk well to make a broken vinaigrette.

Fry the ginger chips. Heat 1 inch of canola oil to 350°F in a small saucepan. Slice the ginger into thin rounds. Fry the ginger until lightly colored and crispy, 1 to 2 minutes. Remove with a slotted spoon and drain on paper towels.

Cut the chilled tuna into ½-inch-thick tiles and arrange on a large platter. Arrange the braised carrots around the tuna, and drizzle the carrots and tuna lightly with the vinaigrette. Garnish with radish sprouts and the crispy ginger.

confit veg

A specialty of Gascony, France, confit is a cooking technique used to preserve a variety of foods, most often meats, which are salted and slowly cooked in their own fat. With vegetables it's a slightly different story, although the concepts share the same theology. A protein confit is about depth of flavor, but a vegetable confit is about a jammy brightness and butter-soft texture.

Confit of root vegetable—it doesn't particularly matter which roots—has a goal: to both intensify the flavor and melt the texture slowly in a controlled situation. Substituting the tough sinew of a pork trotter or a duck leg with the coarse fiber and density of a raw beet or a large carrot is a wash from a technical standpoint. I simply replace duck fat with grapeseed oil, garlic and herbs with citrus peel and coriander seed.

SHAVED BABY CARROTS, ROSE YOGURT, FENUGREEK, POMEGRANATE, AND MINT

SERVES 4

POMEGRANATE PEARLS
2 cups olive oil
½ cup unsweetened 100% pomegranate juice
3.5 grams agar agar powder

6 young red, yellow, and/or orange carrots

ROSE YOGURT
1 cup plain 2% Greek yogurt
1 tablespoon orange blossom honey
1 tablespoon rose water
1 teaspoon fresh lemon juice
½ teaspoon ground fenugreek
Kosher salt

2 tablespoons crushed lightly toasted pistachios
2 tablespoons fresh mint leaves
Ground fenugreek
¼ cup organic rose petals
¼ cup micro cilantro

Make the pomegranate pearls. Pour the olive oil into a tall glass and place it in the freezer for about 30 minutes to chill to 38°F. In a small saucepan, combine the pomegranate juice with the agar agar and whisk well. Set over medium heat and bring to a simmer to dissolve the agar completely. Remove from the heat and chill in the refrigerator for 5 minutes. Fill a large plastic syringe or a plastic squeeze bottle with a neatly trimmed tip with the pomegranate juice, and carefully dispense large drops into the chilled olive oil, creating gel pearls. Leave to firm up for a few minutes. Drain the pearls when ready to use, reserving the olive oil for another use.

Prepare the carrots. Peel the carrots and use a mandoline to slice them lengthwise into long thin strips. Place in a large bowl of ice water to crisp and curl up.

Prepare the rose yogurt. In a blender, combine the yogurt with the honey, rose water, lemon juice, fenugreek, and salt. Blend until a layer of foam rises to the top.

Drain the carrots and serve with the pistachios, mint leaves, and a sprinkle of fenugreek. Use a spoon to drizzle each salad with rose yogurt foam. Garnish with the rose petals, cilantro, and pomegranate gel pearls.

ROASTED CAULIFLOWER WITH ANCHOVY, CAPERS, AND FRESH THYME

SERVES 4 TO 6

CAULIFLOWER

2 heads cauliflower (preferably different colors)
Extra-virgin olive oil
Kosher salt and freshly cracked black pepper

GARLIC CHIPS

Olive oil, for frying
3 garlic cloves, thinly sliced

1 tablespoon extra-virgin olive oil
3 oil-packed anchovy fillets, finely minced
2 garlic cloves, finely minced
1 tablespoon salt-packed capers, rinsed
    and drained
4 sprigs fresh thyme, leaves only
½ cup heavy cream
¼ cup grated Parmigiano-Reggiano
½ lemon
Freshly cracked black pepper
Shaved Parmigiano-Reggiano

Roast the cauliflower. Preheat the oven to 450°F. Remove the green leaves from the cauliflower and reserve. Cut the cauliflower heads in half, then into bite-size florets. Cut the stalks into bite-size pieces also. Place the florets and stalk pieces in a roasting pan, and drizzle with olive oil and season with salt and pepper. Roast until golden and tender, about 20 minutes. Transfer to a platter lined with paper towels to drain.

Make the garlic chips. Pour ¼ inch of oil into a small saucepan. Add the garlic and set the pan over medium heat. Heat the oil until the chips are golden and crisp, about 1 minute. Drain on paper towels and set aside.

Make the anchovy sauce. Set a large skillet over medium-high heat. Add the olive oil and fry the anchovies, garlic, capers, and thyme, stirring with a wooden spoon to break up the anchovies and infuse the oil. Cook for 3 to 4 minutes, until fragrant. Add the cream and Parmesan, and bring to a simmer. Just before serving, add the roasted cauliflower pieces and fold in the reserved leaves. Finish with a squeeze of lemon juice, and top with the fried garlic chips, cracked black pepper, and shaved Parmesan.

CAULIFLOWER SOUP, CRISPY BRUSSELS SPROUTS, AND SMOKY SALMON ROE

SERVES 4

1 ounce salmon roe
1 teaspoon smoked extra-virgin olive oil

CAULIFLOWER SOUP
3 cups cauliflower florets (about 1 small head)
½ white onion, coarsely chopped
2 sprigs fresh lemon thyme
1½ quarts whole milk
Kosher salt

BRUSSELS SPROUTS
Extra-virgin olive oil
6 or 7 Brussels sprouts, separated into
　　individual leaves
Fleur de sel

1 tablespoon finely chopped fresh chives
1 teaspoon fresh lemon thyme buds
Flaky sea salt and freshly cracked black pepper
Smoked extra-virgin olive oil

In a small nonreactive dish, stir together the salmon roe and smoked olive oil. Set aside to infuse the roe with smoky flavor.

Prepare the cauliflower. Place the cauliflower florets in a large pot with the onion, lemon thyme sprigs, and milk. Slowly bring to a boil over medium-high heat. Season with salt, cover, and simmer for 25 to 30 minutes, until the cauliflower is soft. Discard the lemon thyme sprigs. Transfer the cauliflower to a blender and puree until completely smooth. Taste, and season with salt and keep warm.

Fry the Brussels sprouts. Fill a medium saucepan with 2 to 3 inches of olive oil, and heat it to 350°F. Fry the Brussels sprout leaves, a few at a time, for 30 to 40 seconds, until browned. Drain on paper towels and season with fleur de sel.

To serve, ladle the soup into shallow bowls and garnish with the fried Brussels sprout leaves. Sprinkle with the chives, smoked salmon roe, and lemon thyme buds, and season with flakes of sea salt, cracked black pepper, and smoked olive oil.

CAULIFLOWER PUDDING AND CRISP BRUSSELS SPROUTS WITH SEA URCHIN, RAISINS, AND CAPERS

SERVES 4 TO 6

RAISINS
1 bunch red seedless grapes

CAULIFLOWER PUDDING
Nonstick cooking spray
2 small heads cauliflower
2 tablespoons unsalted butter
1 quart heavy cream
7 large egg yolks
Kosher salt and freshly cracked black pepper

BRUSSELS SPROUTS
6 to 8 Brussels sprouts
3 tablespoons salt-packed capers, rinsed
    and drained
¼ cup raw pine nuts
Extra-virgin olive oil
Kosher salt and freshly cracked black pepper

12 pieces fresh sea urchin (uni)
2 tablespoons chopped fresh chives
1 tablespoon fresh chervil leaves
2 to 3 teaspoons smoked extra-virgin olive oil
Flaky sea salt

Prepare the raisins. Preheat the oven to 300°F. Remove the grapes from the stems and spread them on a baking sheet. Roast for 4 hours, or until shrunken and dehydrated. Cool and set aside.

Prepare the cauliflower. Increase the oven temperature to 325°F and bring a large pot of salted water to a boil. Grease a deep 3-quart baking dish with nonstick cooking spray. Break the cauliflower heads into bite-size florets. Blanch the cauliflower for 3 to 4 minutes, until tender. Drain well.

Make the cauliflower pudding. Place half of the blanched cauliflower in a food processor and add the butter, cream, and egg yolks. Puree until smooth. Season with salt and a touch of pepper, then puree once more. Pour into the prepared baking dish. Set the baking dish inside a roasting pan and fill the larger pan with water to reach three-quarters up the side of the dish. Bake the pudding for 30 to 35 minutes, until set. Cool to room temperature, then chill overnight in the refrigerator. Bring to room temperature before serving.

Roast the Brussels sprouts. Preheat the oven to 375°F. Separate the sprouts into individual leaves. Scatter the remaining cauliflower florets on a baking sheet along with the Brussels sprout leaves, capers, and pine nuts. Drizzle with olive oil and season with salt and pepper. Roast for 15 to 20 minutes, until the vegetables are lightly browned around the edges.

Serve spoonfuls of the cauliflower pudding garnished with pieces of sea urchin. Scatter roasted cauliflower florets, Brussels sprout leaves, pine nuts, and capers around each portion, and add the raisins, chives, and chervil. Drizzle with a little smoked olive oil and season with flaky sea salt.

FROZEN CHOCOLATE RASPBERRY "BOMBS"

SERVES 4 TO 6

3 cups firm but ripe raspberries (about 40 total)
1 cup heavy cream
¼ teaspoon vanilla extract
1 tablespoon confectioners' sugar

½ pound dark chocolate chips
½ cup dark chocolate–covered cacao nibs
Fleur de sel

Fill the berries. Lay the raspberries out on paper towels and sort through them, discarding any soft or damaged berries. Whip the cream until soft peaks form, then add the vanilla and confectioners' sugar. Whip until firm. Using the tip of a paring knife, fill each raspberry with vanilla cream. Then set them out on a tray and freeze for 15 to 20 minutes, until firm.

Coat the "bombs." Line a flat tray with waxed paper; set aside. Melt the dark chocolate chips in a double boiler (or in the microwave). Using toothpicks to hold the raspberries, dip the berries in the dark chocolate so they are completely coated. Work quickly so the cream doesn't melt. Allow the excess chocolate to drip off, and then set the berries on the prepared tray. Repeat dipping the berries until a thick coating of chocolate has formed. Remove the toothpicks, and while the chocolate is still soft, sprinkle the berries lightly with cacao nibs and fleur de sel so they stick to the berries. Freeze the raspberries until firm and serve cold.

CHOCOLATE CAKE, ALMOND ICE CREAM, CARAMEL, AND THYME

SERVES 6

ALMOND ICE CREAM
1½ cups whole milk
1½ cups heavy cream
6 egg yolks
½ cup sugar
1 tablespoon amaretto
1 teaspoon almond extract

CARAMEL
2 cups sugar
¼ cup toasted almonds
⅓ cup heavy cream
4 teaspoons baking soda, sifted

CHOCOLATE CAKE
Nonstick cooking spray
1 pound bittersweet chocolate, chopped
   into small pieces
½ cup (1 stick) unsalted butter
9 large eggs, separated
¾ cup plus 1 tablespoon sugar

1 cup crème fraîche, whipped
1 tablespoon fresh thyme buds
Fleur de sel

Make the ice cream. Combine the milk and cream in a medium saucepan and set over medium heat. Bring to a gentle simmer so bubbles form on the surface, then reduce the heat to low. In a large bowl, combine the egg yolks and sugar. Whisk together until the mixture turns pale yellow. While constantly whisking, pour about half of the hot milk mixture into the egg mixture. Then pour the egg and milk mixture back into the saucepan and cook over low heat, stirring constantly, until the mixture coats the back of a spoon, about 8 minutes. Set a large bowl over ice and pour the ice cream base through a strainer into the bowl. Stir in the amaretto and the almond extract, and set aside to cool completely. Once cool, process in an ice cream maker; then place in the freezer to chill.

Prepare the caramel. Line a rimmed sheet tray with a silicone mat or parchment paper; set aside. In a large saucepan, combine the sugar and ¼ cup of water. Set over high heat, bring to a boil, and simmer until the caramel turns a deep amber. Use a candy thermometer to measure the temperature of the caramel, and when it reaches 260°F (hard ball stage), remove from the heat. Add the almonds and stir well so they toast lightly. Then add the cream and stir well. Transfer 2 to 3 tablespoons of the caramel to a small bowl and set it aside. Once the caramel in the saucepan is hot and bubbling again, add the baking soda—take care, as the mixture will bubble up vigorously. Stir well, and then pour the caramel out onto the lined sheet tray. Allow to sit in a dry place until hardened; then break into bite-size pieces. Store in an airtight container if not using immediately.

Bake the cakes. Preheat the oven to 350°F. Line a sheet tray with parchment or a silicone mat. Lightly spray six 3-inch ring molds with nonstick cooking spray and set them out on the tray. Put the chocolate and butter in the top of a double boiler (or in a heatproof bowl) and heat over about 1 inch of simmering water until melted. Meanwhile, whisk the egg yolks with the sugar in a mixing bowl until pale yellow. Whisk a little of the chocolate mixture into the egg yolk mixture to temper the eggs (this will keep the eggs from scrambling from the heat of the chocolate); then whisk in the rest of the chocolate mixture. Beat the egg whites in another mixing bowl until stiff peaks form, and fold into the chocolate mixture. Pour the cake batter into the prepared ring molds, and bake until the cakes are set, the tops are starting to crack, and a toothpick inserted into the center of a cake comes out with moist crumbs clinging to it, 15 to 17 minutes. Let stand for 5 minutes, then unmold.

To assemble, top the warm chocolate cakes with pieces of caramel. Serve with quenelles of almond ice cream, drizzle with the caramel, and dot each plate with whipped crème fraîche. Garnish with a scattering of thyme buds and fleur de sel.

ROCKY ROAD CHOCOLATE MOUSSE

SERVES 4 TO 6

CHOCOLATE MOUSSE

6 ounces semisweet chocolate, chopped
3 tablespoons unsalted butter, softened
3 large eggs, separated
½ teaspoon cream of tartar
¼ cup plus 2 tablespoons sugar
½ cup cold heavy cream
½ teaspoon vanilla extract

RAISINS

2 cups California red seedless grapes

BRIOCHE

1 brioche roll
Extra-virgin olive oil

CANDIED ORANGE SLICES

½ cup sugar
1 navel orange, cut into ¼-inch-thick slices

2 cups buttered popcorn, lightly salted
1 cup salted roasted cashews
Fresh mint buds
Fleur de sel
Extra-virgin olive oil

Make the chocolate mousse. Put a medium mixing bowl in the refrigerator to chill. Bring about 1 inch of water to a simmer in a saucepan; put the chocolate and butter in a medium heat-proof bowl and set it over the pan, making sure that it doesn't touch the water. Stir with a wooden spoon until the chocolate is melted and the mixture is smooth.

Remove the bowl from the heat and let the mixture cool slightly. Then whisk the egg yolks into the chocolate one at a time, beating until smooth after each addition. Set aside. In a separate bowl, whisk the egg whites until foamy. Add the cream of tartar and beat until soft peaks form. Gradually beat in the ¼ cup sugar and continue beating until stiff peaks form. In the chilled mixing bowl, beat the heavy cream until it begins to thicken up. Add the remaining 2 tablespoons sugar and the vanilla, and continue beating until the cream holds soft peaks.

Now combine the three mixtures: Stir a spoonful of the egg whites into the chocolate mixture to lighten it; then fold in the rest. Fold in the whipped cream, taking care not to overwork the mousse. Chill in the refrigerator for 1 to 2 hours.

Prepare the raisins. Reduce the oven temperature to 200°F. Spread the grapes out on a roasting tray and bake them in the oven for 2 hours. Remove and set aside to cool.

Toast the brioche. Preheat the oven to 350°F. Thinly slice the brioche roll, place the slices on a sheet tray, and drizzle them with olive oil. Bake in the oven until golden brown, 7 to 8 minutes. Set aside and allow to cool.

Candy the orange slices. In a medium saucepan, combine the sugar and 1½ cups of water and bring to a boil over high heat. Add the orange slices and return to a boil. Then reduce the heat to medium and simmer, turning the oranges occasionally, until the liquid has reduced to a thin syrup and the oranges have turned translucent, about 25 minutes. When done, the orange slices will be tender and the sauce will be thick like a glaze. Transfer the oranges to a tray lined with waxed paper and allow to cool.

To assemble the rocky road, smear chocolate mousse on the center of each plate. Top with raisins, popcorn, cashews, and brioche toast. Garnish with mint buds and orange slices, and season with fleur de sel and olive oil.

SMOKY ROASTED CHICKEN AND CITRUS SALSA

SERVES 2 TO 4

CHICKEN
1 whole (3½-pound) free-range chicken
½ cup smoked olive oil
Kosher salt and freshly cracked black pepper

1½ pounds baby creamer potatoes
    in assorted colors

CITRUS SALSA
2 limes
1 navel orange
1 grapefruit
Extra-virgin olive oil
Kosher salt and freshly cracked black pepper
6 breakfast radishes
3 tablespoons finely chopped fresh chives

Flowering cilantro buds
Fleur de sel

Roast the chicken. Preheat the oven to 375°F. Using a sharp knife or kitchen shears, cut along both sides of the backbone and discard it. Flatten the chicken and cut it in half through the breast so you have two halves—each with a leg and breast. Rub all over with some of the smoked olive oil, ensuring it gets in all the crevices. Season all over with salt and pepper.

Set the chicken in a large roasting pan over two burners and heat over medium-high heat. When the pan is hot, add the chicken halves skin-side down and sear for 4 to 5 minutes. Turn the chicken over, add the potatoes to the pan, and drizzle with more smoked olive oil. Season with salt and pepper. Roast in the oven for 45 minutes, or until an instant-read thermometer inserted in the joint between the thigh and drumstick reads 160° to 165°F. The potatoes should be golden on the outside and tender in the middle. Remove from the oven and allow the chicken to rest for 5 minutes.

Make the citrus salsa. Use a sharp knife to cut away the rind and pith from each of the citrus fruits. Holding the fruit over a bowl, carefully cut between the membranes to free the segments. Let the juices and segments fall into the bowl. Add about ¼ cup extra-virgin olive oil to the bowl and season with salt and pepper. Cut the radishes into very fine matchsticks on a mandoline or with a sharp knife. Fold them into the citrus salsa, and add the chives.

Serve the roasted chicken with the potatoes and citrus salsa, and garnish with flowering cilantro. Season with fleur de sel.

WILD ARUGULA, CALIFORNIA GRAPEFRUIT, AND PINE NUT PAVLOVA

SERVES 4 TO 6

PAVLOVA
1½ cups superfine sugar
4 large egg whites
¼ teaspoon cream of tartar
1½ teaspoons vanilla extract
Pinch sea salt
1 teaspoon crushed pink peppercorns
¾ cup toasted pine nuts

1 grapefruit
1 teaspoon pink peppercorns
2 cups fresh baby arugula
2 to 3 tablespoons grapefruit olive oil
    (such as "O" grapefruit olive oil)
2 tablespoons aged balsamic vinegar

Make the pavlova. Pour 1 cup of water into a saucepan, add the superfine sugar, and bring to a simmer. Stir until the sugar has completely dissolved and heat until the syrup reaches 248°F on a candy thermometer. When the syrup is almost up to temperature, use an electric mixer to beat the egg whites to stiff peaks. Beat in the cream of tartar. With the mixer on medium speed, gradually pour in the hot sugar syrup and continue beating until cool. Beat in the vanilla and add the pinch of sea salt.

Preheat the oven to 250°F. Line 2 baking sheets with parchment paper or silicone mats. Spoon half the meringue mixture onto each sheet and spread it into several 1- to 2-inch-wide strips with an offset spatula. Sprinkle lightly with the crushed pink peppercorns and toasted pine nuts. Bake for 10 to 12 minutes, until the outsides of the meringue are set and crisp. Remove the baking sheets from the oven, and while still warm, carefully remove the pavlova strips and form them into shapes by laying them over a rolling pin or carefully twisting. Place the twisted pavlova pieces back on the baking sheets and return to the oven. With the heat off and the oven door ajar, allow the pavlovas to cool completely, 2 to 3 hours. Transfer to a wire rack.

Prepare the citrus. Using a sharp knife, slice away the rind and pith from the grapefruit. Cut between the membranes to free each segment.

Serve the pavlova pieces with the grapefruit supremes, pink peppercorns, and arugula. Dot with the grapefruit olive oil and balsamic vinegar.

POACHED SALMON, GRAINS, GRAPEFRUIT, AND CHILE

SERVES 4

GRAPEFRUIT MAYO
2 egg whites
¼ teaspoon Dijon mustard
2 tablespoons fresh lemon juice
1 teaspoon grated grapefruit zest
¼ teaspoon kosher salt
¼ teaspoon sugar
1 cup grapeseed oil

GRAINS
1 cup wheat berries, rinsed
3 lemongrass stalks, trimmed to 5 inches
    and smashed
½ cup red quinoa
½ cup white quinoa
Kosher salt and freshly cracked black pepper
½ cup couscous
¼ cup fresh grapefruit juice
¼ cup extra-virgin olive oil

SALMON
2 (6-inch) lemongrass stalks, bashed
2 (12-ounce) boneless, skinless salmon fillets

2 grapefruits
Fleur de sel
¼ cup chopped roasted Jimmy Nardello
    peppers, crushed to a pulp with a mortar
    and pestle and a little olive oil
Fresh basil
Fresh fennel fronds
Fresh thyme

Make the grapefruit mayo. In a blender, combine the egg whites, mustard, lemon juice, grapefruit zest, salt, and sugar. Blend until combined. With the blender running, add the grapeseed oil in a slow, steady stream so the mixture emulsifies. Refrigerate until ready to serve.

Cook the grains. Place the wheat berries in a pot with 2 cups of water and 1 lemongrass stalk. Bring to a boil. Then reduce the heat and simmer for 1 to 1½ hours, until the grains are tender and chewy. Drain and set aside.

Place the red and white quinoa in a saucepan and add 2 cups of water and another lemongrass stalk. Season with salt. Bring to a boil. Then reduce the heat and simmer for 15 to 17 minutes, until tender. Transfer to a plate and set aside.

Place the couscous in a large heatproof mixing bowl. Combine ⅔ cup of water with the third lemongrass stalk in a saucepan, bring to a boil, then pour the hot water and lemongrass over the couscous. Cover and let sit for 5 minutes.

Discard all 3 lemongrass stalks, and add the wheat berries and quinoa to the couscous in the mixing bowl. Dress with the grapefruit juice and olive oil. Season with salt and pepper.

Steam the salmon. Fill a large pot with 2 inches of water and set over high heat. Place a steamer basket inside and lay the 2 bashed lemongrass stalks on the basket. Arrange the salmon fillets across the lemongrass. Reduce the heat so the water is simmering gently. Cover the pot with a lid or foil to trap the steam, and cook for 2 to 3 minutes, until the salmon is pale pink all over. Transfer the salmon to a plate and chill in the fridge. Once cooled, flake the salmon into large pieces.

Prepare the citrus. Use a sharp knife to slice off the rind and pith from the grapefruits. Cut between the membranes to free the grapefruit segments.

Serve the cooled salmon over the mixed grains, garnished with the grapefruit segments and grapefruit mayo. Season with fleur de sel and garnish with the peppers, basil, fennel fronds, and thyme.

CALIFORNIA GRAPES AND PARSLEY-LIME GRANITA

SERVES 4

The granita is like a frozen vinaigrette for this salad.

LIME GRANITA
¾ cup sugar
2 cups lightly packed flat-leaf parsley
1 cup fresh lime juice
½ teaspoon grated lime zest

2 limes
3 cups red seedless grapes
2 cups lightly packed flat-leaf parsley
Extra-virgin olive oil
Fleur de sel and freshly cracked black pepper

Make the granita. Combine the sugar and 2 cups of water in a saucepan and set over medium heat. Bring to a boil and stir until the sugar has dissolved. Remove from the heat, and add the parsley, lime juice, and lime zest. The parsley will turn bright green from the heat. Allow to cool slightly, then transfer to a blender and puree. Pass through a cheesecloth-lined strainer into a shallow dish, cover, and place in the freezer. Freeze for 2 hours or until just barely set. Then use a spoon to scrape the frozen granita into light, airy shavings.

Prepare the fruit. Using a sharp knife, slice away the rind and pith from each lime. Cut between the membranes to free each segment. Place the supremes in a large mixing bowl.

Cut the grapes in half through the equator and add to the bowl along with the parsley. Drizzle with olive oil and season lightly with fleur de sel and pepper. Serve mounds of the parsley and grape salad dotted with spoonfuls of the lime granita.

KEY LIME PIE

ITALIAN MERINGUE

1 cup superfine sugar
5 egg whites, at room temperature
¼ teaspoon cream of tartar

GRAHAM CRACKER CRUMBS

4 tablespoons (½ stick) unsalted butter
10 graham crackers
1 teaspoon ground cinnamon
3 tablespoons turbinado sugar
Pinch kosher salt

LIME CURD FILLING

6 egg yolks
1 cup sugar
Grated zest and juice of 4 limes
¼ teaspoon vanilla extract
½ cup (1 stick) unsalted butter, cut into chunks
¼ cup flat-leaf parsley leaves

2 limes
2 to 3 tablespoons flat-leaf parsley leaves

Make the meringue. Line a rimmed sheet tray with a silicone mat or parchment paper; set aside. Preheat the oven to 200°F. In a small pot over medium heat, combine the sugar and ⅓ cup of water. Gently swirl the pot over the burner to dissolve the sugar completely. Do not stir. Raise the heat and boil the mixture to the soft ball stage (235° to 240°F)—use a candy thermometer for accuracy. While the sugar syrup is heating, whip the egg whites: In the bowl of a stand mixer fitted with the whisk attachment, whip the eggs whites on low speed until foamy. Add the cream of tartar, increase the speed to medium, and beat until soft peaks form. With the mixer running, pour the hot sugar syrup in a thin stream down the side of the bowl. Once all the sugar syrup has been added, raise the speed to high and beat until the egg whites are stiff and glossy, 6 to 7 minutes. Using an offset spatula, spread the meringue mixture out on the lined sheet tray so it is about ½ inch thick. Bake in the oven for 1 hour, until the meringue is set but still tender. Finish with a brûlée torch to brown the top of the meringue. Break the meringue into bite-size pieces and set aside until ready to assemble the dessert.

Prepare the graham cracker crumbs. Place the butter in a small saucepan and set it over medium-high heat. Melt the butter and then cook until it is foamy, browned, and fragrant, 2 to 3 minutes. Place the graham crackers in a food processor and pulse until crumbled. Add the cinnamon, sugar, and melted butter, and pulse again. Season with the pinch of salt.

Make the lime curd. Set a medium pot of water over high heat and bring to a simmer. Combine the egg yolks, sugar, lime zest, and lime juice in a metal or heat-resistant glass bowl and whisk until smooth. Set the bowl over the simmering water, without letting the bottom touch the water, and whisk vigorously for 7 to 8 minutes, until the curd has doubled in volume and is starting to get thick and creamy. Don't let it boil or the yolks will scramble. Remove the bowl from the heat and whisk in the vanilla and the butter, a couple of chunks at a time, until melted. Put the parsley leaves in the container of a blender. Pour in the lime curd and blend on high speed until the parsley is completely pureed and the mixture is thick and creamy. Cool the mixture to room temperature.

Prepare the citrus. Using a sharp knife, slice away the rind and pith from each lime. Cut in between the membranes to free each segment.

To assemble, smear ½ cup of the lime curd in the bottom of each shallow bowl or plate. Chill the plates in the refrigerator for 10 to 15 minutes, until the curd has set. Top with pieces of meringue, the graham cracker mixture, fresh parsley leaves, and lime supremes.

CALIFORNIA CLAM CHOWDER

SERVES 4

2 thick slices sourdough bread
1 pint Brussels sprouts
6 slices applewood-smoked bacon
8 to 10 small purple creamer potatoes
2 garlic cloves, thinly sliced
1 pint cherry tomatoes on the vine
½ cup extra-virgin olive oil
Kosher salt and freshly cracked black pepper

CHILE OIL

1 tablespoon dried red pepper flakes
2 sprigs fresh lemon thyme
½ cup extra-virgin olive oil
Kosher salt

CLAMS

32 littleneck clams
3 garlic cloves, crushed
2 bay leaves
6 sprigs fresh lemon thyme
3 tablespoons unsalted butter
2 cups heavy cream
Kosher salt and freshly cracked black pepper

Preheat the oven to 350°F. In a food processor, pulse the bread slices to make large, coarse bread crumbs. Slice the Brussels sprouts in half through the stem. Slice the bacon strips on a severe bias to create long, thin lardons. On a large baking sheet combine the potatoes, Brussels sprouts, sliced garlic cloves, bread crumbs, tomatoes, and bacon. Drizzle with the olive oil and season well with salt and pepper. Roast for 25 to 30 minutes, until the potatoes are tender and the bacon and bread crumbs are crisped. Remove from the oven and keep warm.

Make the chile oil. Combine the red pepper flakes and lemon thyme with the olive oil in a small saucepan. Set over medium heat and warm through to infuse. Heat, but don't allow to bubble, for 8 to 10 minutes. Then remove from the heat and season with salt.

Cook the clams. In a large stockpot, combine the clams, crushed garlic cloves, bay leaves, lemon thyme, butter, and 1 cup of water. Cover with a lid and bring to a boil over high heat. Steam the clams for 12 to 15 minutes, until all have opened, discarding any that remain closed. Transfer the clams to a plate. Boil the liquid over high heat for about 5 minutes, until slightly thickened and reduced. Add the cream and season with salt and pepper. Return the clams to the pot and mix well.

Divide the clams among 4 shallow bowls. Arrange the roasted potatoes, Brussels sprouts, tomatoes, bacon, garlic, and bread crumbs over the clams. Pour some creamy clam broth into each bowl and finish with a drizzle of chile oil. Garnish with the lemon thyme and bay leaves from the pot.

clams

In 2007, a British scientific team from Bangor University's School of Ocean Sciences discovered a live arctic quahog clam estimated to be 405 years old. Each summer when the water is warmer, clams grow a 0.1-millimeter layer of shell. When the ancient clam shell was cut in half and the layers counted, similar to counting the rings of a tree, they discovered that the clam was the oldest living animal on earth. The discovery sparked a study on aging by the same university in which scientists concluded that clams had a high resistance to oxidative stress. In humans, oxidative stress is the cellular wear and tear on our bodies as we get older and it increasingly has been implicated as the underlying pathogenic mechanism of a wide range of age-related diseases. As science discovers more and more the connection between a healthy diet and longevity, we've begun to realize that optimizing our nutrition intake with foods naturally high in antioxidants is a powerful way to age gracefully and stay healthy.

CRISP CORNMEAL OYSTERS, CELERY ROOT RÉMOULADE, AND PRESERVED LEMON

SERVES 4 TO 6

RÉMOULADE

½ medium celery root
Juice of 2 lemons
2 egg whites
3 tablespoons Dijon mustard
¼ teaspoon kosher salt
1 tablespoon white wine vinegar
1 cup grapeseed oil
1 tablespoon finely chopped cornichons
2 teaspoons finely chopped capers
1 teaspoon finely chopped flat-leaf parsley
2 teaspoons finely chopped fresh chives
2 teaspoons finely chopped fresh tarragon
Kosher salt and freshly cracked black pepper

QUICK PRESERVED LEMON

2 lemons
2 tablespoons kosher salt
2 tablespoons sugar
1 teaspoon lightly toasted yellow mustard seeds
¼ teaspoon fennel seeds
1 bay leaf

OYSTERS

24 West Coast oysters (such as Hog Island,
    Tomales Bay, Drakes Bay)
1½ cups buttermilk
Vegetable oil, for deep frying
1½ cups medium-grind yellow cornmeal
1 tablespoon garlic powder
Kosher salt and freshly cracked black pepper

½ celery root, peeled and julienned
Fresh fennel fronds, parsley, and tarragon

Make the rémoulade. Bring a large pot of salted water to a boil. Working quickly, peel the celery root and dice into small cubes. Add the juice of 1 lemon to the water (this prevents the celery root from turning brown), then add the celery root. Blanch the cubes for 1 minute, until just tender, then drain well and set aside to cool.

In a blender, combine the egg whites, mustard, salt, remaining lemon juice, and vinegar. Then, with the blender running, slowly pour in the grapeseed oil to emulsify. Thin with a tablespoon or two of water, then pour into a large mixing bowl. Add the celery root, cornichons, capers, parsley, chives, and tarragon. Season with salt and pepper and mix well.

Make the preserved lemon. Thinly slice the lemons. Set a pot of water over high heat. Blanch the lemon slices in the hot water for 30 seconds to soften. Drain and allow to cool. In a small saucepan combine the salt, sugar, mustard seeds, fennel seeds, and bay leaf. Add a touch of water to dissolve. Then add the lemon slices and toss to coat evenly. Arrange the lemon slices flat in a vacuum-seal bag. Seal the bag on the highest pressure setting and set aside until ready to use.

Make the oysters. Shuck the oysters. Combine the oysters and buttermilk in a small bowl and marinate for 15 to 20 minutes. Fill a large pot with 2 to 3 inches of vegetable oil, set it over medium-high heat, and heat it to 350°F. Mix the cornmeal with the garlic powder, and season with salt and pepper. Working in batches of 2 or 3, drain the oysters, dredge them in the cornmeal mixture, then fry them, turning once, for 3 to 4 minutes, until golden brown. Drain on paper towels and season immediately with salt.

Arrange the julienned celery root on each plate. Top with rémoulade and 4 to 6 oysters. Dress with the preserved lemon slices and garnish with fennel fronds and herbs.

DUNGENESS CRAB WITH SRIRACHA DRESSING, LEMONGRASS JELLY, PICKLED MANGO, AND BASIL

SERVES 4

LEMONGRASS JELLY
4 large lemongrass stalks, entire stalk cut into
　¼-inch-thick rounds
1 lime, sliced
½ lemon, sliced
3 tablespoons sugar
1 teaspoon rice vinegar
Pinch kosher salt
4 envelopes powdered gelatin
½ cup lightly packed Thai basil leaves
Grapeseed oil

PICKLED MANGO
2 tablespoons sugar
2 tablespoons fresh lemon juice
2 firm but ripe mangos

FRIED SHALLOT
Canola oil, for shallow frying
1 shallot
½ cup all-purpose flour
Kosher salt

1 pound jumbo lump Dungeness crab meat
2 tablespoons mayonnaise
2 tablespoons sour cream
1 teaspoon Sriracha sauce
Kosher salt
1 serrano chile, finely sliced
Extra-virgin olive oil
Fresh Thai basil buds
Micro cilantro

Make the lemongrass jelly. Set a large pot over high heat. Add 4 cups of water and the lemongrass, lime, lemon, sugar, vinegar, and salt. Bring to a boil, then reduce the heat, cover partially, and simmer for 30 minutes. When done, transfer 1 cup of the strained liquid to a large bowl and allow to cool. Add the gelatin powder and mix thoroughly to soften. Stir back into the main pot and whisk well to incorporate the gelatin. Remove the pot from the heat and add the Thai basil leaves. Leave the liquid to steep for 15 minutes. Then strain the liquid, and discard the aromatics and any lumps of gelatin. Lightly coat a rimmed flat dish with grapeseed oil. Pour the lemongrass jelly into the dish, cover, and refrigerate overnight.

Make the pickled mango. In a small saucepan, combine 1 cup of water, the sugar, and the lemon juice. Bring to a simmer to dissolve the sugar, then remove from the heat and allow to cool. Peel the mangos and slice the flesh off the seed. Cut the flesh into neat ½-inch cubes. Place the cubes and the pickling liquid in a vacuum-sealed bag and seal on the highest compression setting. Set aside until ready to use.

Fry the shallot. Fill a small saucepan with 1 inch of canola oil and place over high heat. Slice the shallot and separate into rings. Lightly dredge the rings in the flour. Drop into the hot oil and fry for 1 to 2 minutes, until golden brown and crispy. Remove with a slotted spoon and drain on paper towels. Season immediately with salt.

Make the crab salad. Pick through the crabmeat and discard any shell or cartilage. In a large mixing bowl, combine the mayonnaise, sour cream, and Sriracha. Season with salt, then gently fold in the crabmeat.

Use a large spoon to scrape out and break up the lemongrass jelly. Serve the crab on a bed of lemongrass jelly, topped with crispy fried shallots, pickled mango, and sliced serrano. Drizzle with some olive oil and garnish with Thai basil buds and some micro cilantro.

DUNGENESS CRAB WITH GREEK YOGURT, CUCUMBER, TOMATO, AND MINT

SERVES 4

CHICKPEAS

2 cups dried chickpeas, soaked overnight
    in water to cover
2 lemon slices
1 bay leaf
Kosher salt
Olive oil, for shallow frying

4 plum tomatoes
1 pound jumbo lump Dungeness crab meat
1 tablespoon fresh lemon juice
¼ cup plain Greek yogurt
Kosher salt and freshly cracked black pepper
2 Persian cucumbers
Fresh mint
Extra-virgin olive oil
Paprika

Make the chickpeas. Drain the chickpeas and place in a medium pot with the lemon, bay leaf, and 1 teaspoon salt. Add water to cover by at least 2 to 3 inches. Bring to a boil over high heat, then reduce the heat and simmer for about 45 minutes, until tender. Drain the chickpeas and pat dry on paper towels. Heat ¼ inch of olive oil in a large sauté pan over medium heat to about 325°F; a chickpea dropped into the oil should sizzle and dance. Add the chickpeas, in batches, and fry for 3 to 5 minutes, until golden and crispy. Drain on paper towels and season with salt while hot.

Prepare the tomatoes. Set a large pot of water over high heat and bring to a boil. Fill a large bowl with ice water. Make a small "x" incision in the bottom of each tomato. Submerge in the hot water for 20 seconds, just until the skin starts to curl back from the cut. Remove with a strainer and transfer immediately to the bowl of ice water. Leave for 10 seconds, then drain and peel off and discard the skins. Quarter the tomatoes, and scoop out and discard the seeds.

Make the crab salad. Pick through the crabmeat and discard any shell or cartilage. In a large mixing bowl, combine the lemon juice with the yogurt and stir well. Gently fold in the crabmeat and season with salt and pepper. Thinly slice the Persian cucumbers. Fold in the tomatoes and cucumbers to dress lightly.

Arrange the tomatoes on 4 plates and top with chunks of crab. Top with the cucumber slices and fried chickpeas, and garnish with the mint. Drizzle with a little olive oil and sprinkle with paprika.

DUCK BREAST, SPICED APPLE PULP, AND WILD RICE CROQUETTES

SERVES 2

SPICED APPLE PULP
3 Honeycrisp apples
Extra-virgin olive oil
Pinch ground cinnamon
Pinch freshly grated nutmeg
Pinch ground cardamom
¼ teaspoon finely chopped fresh rosemary
Kosher salt and freshly cracked black pepper

CROQUETTES
Extra-virgin olive oil
1 Honeycrisp apple, peeled and diced
¼ cup sliced onion
Kosher salt and freshly cracked black pepper
1½ cups cooked wild rice
½ pound loose pork sausage
1 garlic clove, minced
¼ teaspoon finely chopped fresh rosemary
1 egg, beaten
⅓ cup heavy cream
Canola oil, for deep frying

DUCK
2 Pekin duck breasts (about 8 ounces each)
Kosher salt and freshly cracked black pepper
1 garlic clove, smashed
½ small onion, roughly chopped
1 carrot, chopped
1 celery rib, chopped
¼ cup Calvados
1½ cups roasted chicken stock
2 tablespoons cold butter, cut into cubes

Fresh rosemary buds
Organic nasturtium clippings
Extra-virgin olive oil
Freshly cracked black pepper

Make the apple pulp. Preheat the oven to 350°F. Core the unpeeled apples and place on a baking sheet. Drizzle with olive oil and roast for 20 minutes, until the apples are puffy and very tender. Place in a food processor with the cinnamon, nutmeg, cardamom, and rosemary. Season with salt and pepper, and puree until almost but not quite smooth.

Make the croquettes. Set a large sauté pan over high heat. Coat with olive oil and add the diced apple. Sauté until golden brown, about 2 minutes. Transfer to a mixing bowl. Return the pan to the heat and add more oil. Add the onions and sauté until well caramelized, 8 to 9 minutes. Season with salt and pepper, then add to the bowl with the wild rice, sausage, garlic, rosemary, onion, egg, and cream. Mix well. Scoop the mixture out by heaping tablespoons and form quenelles. Refrigerate for 30 minutes to firm up.

Preheat the oven to 200°F. Heat a few inches of canola oil to 375°F in a large deep pot. Working in small batches, deep-fry the croquettes for 5 to 6 minutes, until golden brown. Season with salt and keep warm in the oven.

Cook the duck. Set a large sauté pan over medium-high heat. Score the duck breasts on the skin side, then season with salt and pepper. Place skin-side down in the pan and cook for 7 to 8 minutes, until the fat has rendered and the skin is super-crisp. Turn the breasts over and cook for 3 to 4 minutes more, for medium-rare. Set aside to rest.

Make the sauce. Remove all but 2 tablespoons of the duck fat from the pan. Add the garlic, onion, carrot, and celery and sauté for 10 to 15 minutes, until the vegetables are starting to break down. Add the Calvados and stir to deglaze the pan for a minute, then add the chicken stock and simmer until reduced by half. Strain out and discard the vegetables. Return the sauce to the heat and bring back to a simmer. Season with salt and pepper. Remove from the heat and swirl in the cold butter cubes until incorporated and glossy.

Serve the sliced duck breast with the croquettes and spiced apple pulp, and garnish with rosemary buds and nasturtium sprigs. Drizzle with the pan sauce and olive oil, and season with plenty of cracked black pepper.

DUCK CONFIT WITH WILD MUSHROOMS AND MISO DRESSING

SERVES 4 TO 6

Duck confit can be made up to a week ahead of time and stored in its oil in the refrigerator.

DUCK CONFIT
4 cups plus 1 teaspoon grapeseed oil
10 black peppercorns
4 whole star anise
4 duck legs (about 2 pounds total)
Kosher salt and freshly cracked black pepper
1 head garlic, cut through the equator
2 bay leaves
6 sprigs fresh thyme
1 strip lemon zest

MUSHROOMS
1 pound mixed wild mushrooms (cremini, oyster, chanterelles, shiitake)
Extra-virgin olive oil
Kosher salt and freshly cracked black pepper

MISO DRESSING
2½ tablespoons white miso paste
3 tablespoons seasoned rice vinegar
½ teaspoon light agave syrup
Squeeze of fresh lemon juice
¼ cup grapeseed oil

1 celery heart (4 or 5 inner ribs)
½ cup fresh or frozen cranberries
¼ cup sugar
1 tablespoon fresh lemon juice
2 to 3 tablespoons celery leaves
¼ cup toasted sunflower seeds
Extra-virgin olive oil

Make the duck confit. Combine the teaspoon of grapeseed oil, peppercorns, and star anise in a large ovenproof pot. Toast over medium heat until fragrant, about 2 minutes. Use a slotted spoon to remove the spices and set them aside.

Preheat the oven to 200°F. Trim excess fat from the duck legs. Season both sides well with salt and pepper, then place skin-side down in the pot. Brown for 5 to 6 minutes, then turn the duck legs over. Add the garlic, bay leaves, thyme, lemon zest, star anise, and peppercorns to the pot. Add about 4 cups of grapeseed oil, ensuring the duck is covered. Cover with a round of parchment paper pressed down onto the oil, then cover the pot with a lid. Place the pot in the oven and cook for 3 hours, until the duck is very tender. Remove the duck from the oil and cover or refrigerate until ready to serve.

Roast the mushrooms. Preheat the oven to 450°F. Clean the mushrooms with a brush, then halve the larger ones. Arrange on a baking sheet and drizzle with olive oil. Season with salt and pepper. Roast for 12 to 15 minutes, until the mushrooms are brown and slightly crisp around the edges.

Make the miso dressing. In a bowl, whisk together the miso, rice vinegar, agave, and lemon juice. While stirring, slowly add the grapeseed oil until emulsified. Keep refrigerated until ready to serve.

Crisp the celery. Use a vegetable peeler to create thin ribbons from the celery ribs. Drop in a bowl of ice water and soak for 5 minutes to crisp and curl the ribbons.

Make the cranberries. Place the cranberries in a small saucepan with the sugar and lemon juice. Add ¾ inch of water and simmer until the cranberries are tender and the sugar has melted, 7 to 8 minutes. The liquid should be syrupy; if not, cook a minute or two longer.

Place a sauté pan over high heat. Separate the duck drumsticks from the thighs and place the pieces skin-side down in the hot pan. Sear for 2 to 3 minutes, turn, and cook 1 minute longer, or until heated through. Serve the browned duck confit pieces with the roasted mushrooms, miso dressing, celery, sunflower seeds, and cranberries. Drizzle with a little of the cranberry syrup and some extra-virgin olive oil.

SIX-MINUTE-AND-TWENTY-FIVE-SECOND EGG, ANCHOVY MAYO, ARUGULA, AND CELERY SALT

SERVES 4

ANCHOVY MAYO
2 egg whites
10 oil-packed anchovy fillets
½ teaspoon Dijon mustard
2 teaspoons fresh lemon juice
¼ teaspoon kosher salt
Freshly cracked black pepper
1 cup grapeseed oil

HOMEMADE CELERY SALT
1 teaspoon celery seeds
2 teaspoons flaky sea salt
2 tablespoons fresh celery leaves

4 large organic free-range eggs
Baby arugula

Make the anchovy mayo. In a blender, combine the egg whites, anchovies, mustard, lemon juice, salt, and pepper. With the blender running, add the grapeseed oil in a slow, steady stream so the mixture emulsifies. Refrigerate until ready to serve.

Make the celery salt. Use a mortar and pestle to combine the celery seeds, sea salt, and celery leaves, crushing them together until well blended.

Boil the eggs. Place the eggs in a large pot of cold water and bring to a boil over high heat. Cook for exactly 6 minutes and 25 seconds from the moment the water starts boiling. When the time is up, remove the eggs from the water and plunge them into a bowl of ice water to stop the cooking process.

Carefully peel the eggs and serve them with the anchovy mayo, arugula, and a light sprinkle of celery salt.

SMOKED EGGS WITH ROASTED BRUSSELS SPROUTS, PARMESAN, AND PANCETTA

SERVES 4

BRUSSELS SPROUTS
1 pound Brussels sprouts, trimmed and halved
1 garlic clove, smashed
4 sprigs fresh thyme
Extra-virgin olive oil
Kosher salt and freshly cracked black pepper

PANCETTA
½ pound pancetta, thinly sliced

SMOKED EGGS
4 eggs (chicken and/or quail eggs)
½ cup applewood smoking chips, soaked
    and drained

PARMESAN DRESSING
2 egg whites
½ teaspoon Dijon mustard
2 teaspoons fresh lemon juice
¼ teaspoon kosher salt
¼ teaspoon sugar
½ cup grated Parmigiano-Reggiano
¼ teaspoon freshly cracked black pepper
1 oil-packed anchovy fillet, minced
1 cup grapeseed oil

Fresh baby spinach leaves

Roast the Brussels sprouts. Preheat the oven to 375°F. On a baking sheet, toss together the Brussels sprouts, garlic, and thyme. Drizzle with olive oil and season with salt and pepper. Roast for 45 minutes, until the sprouts are well charred on the outside and edges. Set aside. Reduce the oven temperature to 325°F.

Cook the pancetta. Spread the pancetta slices on a baking sheet. Bake in the 325°F oven for 15 to 20 minutes, until crisp.

Boil the eggs. Place a large pot of cold water over high heat. Add the eggs to the cold water and just as the water becomes warm (110° to 115°F), start a timer for 6 minutes and 30 seconds. When done, remove the eggs, run them under cold water, and peel. Using a cold smoker (or smoker gun), smoke the eggs over the applewood chips for 15 minutes (see Note). When done, cut the eggs in half lengthwise.

Make the Parmesan dressing. In a blender, combine the egg whites, mustard, lemon juice, salt, sugar, Parmesan, pepper, and anchovy. Blend until smooth. With the blender running, add the grapeseed oil in a slow, steady stream so the mixture emulsifies. Refrigerate until ready to use.

Serve the Brussels sprouts with the smoked eggs and crisp pancetta. Dress with the Parmesan dressing and garnish with baby spinach leaves.

NOTE If you don't have a smoker, you can improvise one: Line a roasting pan with foil, place the soaked chips in the bottom, and set on the stovetop over high heat until the chips begin to smolder. Then set a rack in the pan and lay the eggs on the rack. Cover the whole pan with foil and position it so the eggs are not over the direct heat—otherwise they will overcook. Smoke for 15 minutes.

quail eggs

I love it when I stumble across great information about ingredients that I've been cooking with for years. As a potential superfood, quail eggs are incredibly promising. Tucked into a tiny speckled shell, quail eggs contain a dense level of nutrition rarely found in a single food source. Quail eggs have a higher protein content than chicken eggs and twice as much vitamins A and B_2, plus they are naturally loaded with both omega-3 and omega-6 heart-healthy fatty acids. Also, the very high level of choline found in quail eggs helps protect the brain's neural signals, which can strengthen memory and perhaps prevent dementia. Concerns about the high cholesterol content of quail eggs led me to dig a little deeper; as it turns out, these concerns may be misplaced. Quail eggs are high in cholesterol, but it's HDL cholesterol, the good kind that cleanses the blood, with virtually no LDL, the bad fat that clogs the arteries of your heart.

BLACK COD, SWEET ROASTED EGGPLANT, LEMON AIOLI, SUNFLOWER, AND FIG

SERVES 4

LEMON AIOLI
2 egg whites
¼ teaspoon Dijon mustard
2 tablespoons fresh lemon juice
½ teaspoon grated lemon zest
¼ teaspoon kosher salt
¼ teaspoon sugar
1 cup grapeseed oil

EGGPLANT
1 large Italian eggplant (about 2 pounds)
⅓ cup extra-virgin olive oil, plus more
    for drizzling
Kosher salt and freshly cracked black pepper
2 tablespoons fresh lemon juice

Grapeseed oil
4 (6-ounce) black cod fillets, boned, skin on
Kosher salt and freshly cracked black pepper
6 ripe California Mission figs, halved
¼ cup sunflower sprouts
Flaky sea salt
½ cup toasted sunflower seeds
1 tablespoon ground fenugreek

Make the lemon aioli. In a blender, combine the egg whites, mustard, lemon juice, lemon zest, salt, and sugar. Blend until combined. With the blender running, add the grapeseed oil in a slow, steady stream so the mixture emulsifies.

Prepare the eggplant puree. Preheat the oven to 400°F. Split the eggplant in half lengthwise through the stem. Using a sharp knife, lightly score the flesh side of each half in a diamond pattern about ½ inch deep; this will help release some of the moisture as the eggplant cooks so the flesh roasts evenly. Drizzle with olive oil and season with salt and pepper. Place cut-side down on a roasting tray and roast for 25 to 30 minutes until very soft. When done, remove from the oven and use a large spoon to scoop out the flesh and place it in a large mixing bowl, discarding the skins. Season well with salt and pepper, and add the lemon juice and ⅓ cup olive oil. Using a potato masher, crush the eggplant pulp until it is well combined but not completely smooth.

Cook the fish. Heat a large sauté pan over high heat and coat with grapeseed oil. Season the cod fillets with salt and pepper and place in the pan, skin-side down. Sear for 7 to 8 minutes, pressing the fillets with the back of a spatula to crisp the skin. Then remove from the heat and flip the fillets over to warm through on the other side for 1 minute.

Spoon some of the eggplant pulp onto each plate and top with the crispy cod fillets, halved figs, and sunflower sprouts. Season with flakes of sea salt, garnish with the toasted sunflower seeds, and dot with the lemon aioli. Finish with a sprinkle of ground fenugreek.

RICOTTA RAVIOLI WITH EGGPLANT CAPONATA, PINE NUTS, AND BASIL

SERVES 4 TO 6

PASTA DOUGH

2 cups all-purpose flour, plus more for dusting
1 teaspoon salt
4 large eggs
2 tablespoons extra-virgin olive oil,
    plus extra for brushing

RAVIOLI FILLING

1½ pounds good-quality fresh ricotta, drained
½ cup finely grated Parmigiano-Reggiano
1 large egg
Pinch grated lemon zest

CAPONATA

About ½ cup extra-virgin olive oil
3 oil-packed anchovy fillets, coarsely chopped
1 teaspoon dried red pepper flakes
3 garlic cloves, minced
1 medium onion, diced
4 Japanese eggplants or 1 large Italian eggplant,
    cut into ¼-inch cubes
¼ cup raisins
3 tablespoons salt-packed capers, rinsed
    and drained
½ cup pitted Kalamata olives
2 tomatoes, halved and seeds squeezed out,
    coarsely chopped
1 red bell pepper, chopped
2 tablespoons balsamic vinegar
Pinch sugar
½ bunch fresh basil, hand-torn
Kosher salt and freshly cracked black pepper

Canola oil, for shallow frying
1 pint cherry tomatoes
¼ cup raw pine nuts
Kosher salt
1 cup caperberries
6 to 8 fresh basil buds
1 to 2 tablespoons fresh ricotta

Make the pasta dough. In an electric mixer fitted with a dough hook, combine the 2 cups flour and the salt. Whisk 3 eggs and the olive oil together in a bowl. With the mixer running, add the egg mixture and beat until it is fully incorporated and the dough forms a ball. Sprinkle some flour on a clean work surface and knead the dough until elastic and smooth; this should take about 10 minutes. Brush the surface of the dough with a little extra olive oil and wrap the dough in plastic wrap; set aside to rest for about 30 minutes.

Make the ravioli filling. In a large bowl, combine the ricotta with the Parmesan, egg, and lemon zest. Whisk together, then cover and refrigerate until ready to use.

Make the caponata. Coat a large sauté pan with olive oil and place it over medium-high heat. Add the anchovies, red pepper flakes, garlic, and onion and sauté until translucent and fragrant, 4 to 5 minutes. Add the eggplant and cook until browned all over — you may need to add more olive oil as the eggplant soaks it up. Add the raisins, capers, olives, tomatoes, bell pepper, balsamic, and sugar, stir, and simmer for 15 to 20 minutes. Finish with the torn fresh basil, and season with salt and pepper. Keep warm.

Form the ravioli. Cut the ball of dough in half. Cover and reserve the piece you are not immediately using to prevent it from drying out. Dust the counter and the dough with a little flour. Press the dough into a rectangle and roll it through a pasta machine 2 or 3 times at the widest setting, pulling and stretching the sheet of dough with the palm of your hand as it emerges from the rollers. Reduce the setting and crank the dough through 2 or 3 more times. Continue tightening until the machine is at the narrowest setting; the dough should be very thin – about ⅛ inch thick (you should be able to just see your hand through it). Dust the sheet of dough with flour as needed. Repeat with the second portion of dough.

Beat the remaining egg with 1 tablespoon of water to make an egg wash. Dust the counter and a sheet of dough with flour. Lay out the sheet of dough and brush the surface with the egg wash, which acts as a glue. Drop tablespoons of the ricotta filling down one long side of the dough sheet, spacing them about 2 inches apart. Fold the other half of the sheet over the filling like a blanket. With an espresso cup or your

TYLER FLORENCE FRESH

fingers, gently press out the air pockets around each mound of filling. Use a 2-inch round cookie cutter to cut the ravioli out. Set the ravioli on a baking sheet and lightly dust with flour to prevent sticking. Repeat with the remaining dough and filling.

Prepare the garnish. Heat 1 inch of canola oil in a large pot over high heat. Add the cherry tomatoes and cook for 3 to 4 seconds so the skins just burst. Set aside. Toast the pine nuts in a dry sauté pan over medium heat until golden brown. Season with salt.

Cook the ravioli. Bring a large pot of salted water to a boil. Add the ravioli, in batches, and cook for 2 to 3 minutes, until they float to the top and puff up slightly. Lift the ravioli from the water with a large strainer or slotted spoon. Place the cooked ravioli in the pan of caponata and swirl it around to lightly coat each piece.

Serve the ravioli with the caponata, roasted cherry tomatoes, toasted pine nuts, caperberries, and fresh basil buds. Spoon some of the caponata oil over and around the plate. Dot with the ricotta.

TANGLE OF RAW VEGETABLES WITH SMOKY EGGPLANT, VADOUVAN, AND LEMON-YOGURT DRESSING

SERVES 2 TO 4

1 large eggplant
1½ tablespoons vadouvan spice blend
2 tablespoons grapeseed oil
2 tablespoons toasted sesame oil
Kosher salt and freshly cracked black pepper

1 butternut squash
2 medium carrots
Stems from 2 heads broccoli

LEMON-YOGURT DRESSING
2 cups plain Greek yogurt
1 tablespoon extra-virgin olive oil
1 teaspoon fresh lemon juice
1 teaspoon grated lemon zest
2 teaspoons light agave syrup
Kosher salt

Cilantro sprouts
Toasted sesame seeds

Prepare the eggplant. Preheat the oven to 350°F. Char the outside of the eggplant over a low flame on a stovetop burner, about 2 minutes per side. Place on a baking sheet and roast in the oven for 25 to 30 minutes. Allow to cool slightly before cutting off and discarding the stem. Cut the eggplant into pieces, skin and all, and place in a food processor. Add the vadouvan and the grapeseed and sesame oils, and season with salt and pepper. Process until smooth.

Prepare the vegetables. Halve the butternut squash, peel it, and remove the seeds. Using a mandoline, slice the squash into long thin julienne strips. Repeat the process with the carrots and broccoli stems. Toss the vegetables together in a large bowl.

Make the lemon-yogurt dressing. Whisk all the dressing ingredients together. Pour over the vegetable strips, tossing lightly to coat, and chill for 30 minutes to soften the vegetables.

Spread some pureed eggplant on each plate. Top with a handful of tangled vegetables. Garnish with cilantro sprouts and toasted sesame seeds.

ENDIVE AND WATERCRESS SALAD WITH PEAR PUREE, BLUE CHEESE, AND HAZELNUTS

SERVES 4

PEAR PUREE
3 firm but ripe Bartlett pears
1 teaspoon fresh lemon juice
1 to 2 teaspoons light agave syrup
Pinch kosher salt

1 cup hazelnuts
Kosher salt

8 to 10 ounces mild blue cheese,
    such as Humboldt Fog
2 heads Belgian endive: 1 red, 1 white
1 bunch hydroponic watercress
Fresh chervil leaves
Extra-virgin olive oil
Flaky sea salt and freshly cracked black pepper

Make the pear puree. Preheat the oven to 400°F. Peel, halve, and core the pears. Place in a large mixing bowl and toss with the lemon juice; this will prevent them from turning brown. Drizzle with the agave (adjust the amount according to how sweet your pears are). Transfer the pears and juices to a baking sheet and roast for 10 to 12 minutes, until tender. Puree in a food processor until smooth, and season with a touch of salt.

Roast the hazelnuts. Preheat the oven to 400°F. Place the hazelnuts in a plastic bag and very gently smash with the bottom of a pan or wine bottle to crack the nuts in half. Spread the nuts evenly on a baking sheet. Roast for 7 to 8 minutes, until golden brown. Season lightly with salt and set aside to cool.

Remove the cheese from the fridge, slice it into 4 wedges, and bring to room temperature.

Make the salad. Wash the endives; separate the leaves. Toss together with the watercress. Mound on plates with a wedge of blue cheese. Dot with the pear puree, and garnish with the hazelnuts and chervil leaves. Drizzle with olive oil, and sprinkle with some sea salt and a few turns of cracked black pepper.

raw milk cheese

Raw milk cheeses reside at the center of the debate on fat consumption vs. probiotic health. The French eat 60 percent more natural, probiotic-rich, raw, unpasteurized cheese than we do here in the United States, yet only 8 percent of the French are considered overweight. The question "How can they consume so much fat and be so healthy at the same time?" is known as the French paradox. First identified in 1819 by Dr. Samuel Black of Dublin, Ireland, the French paradox refers to the low rate of coronary heart disease in France despite a diet rich in saturated fats. French researchers suggest that it's the relationship we have with milk that is the problem, not the cheese. Through clinical trials conducted on lab rats eating Camembert, Dr. Serge Renault discovered that as a result of the fermentation process the calcium in cheese neutralizes the fat and combines with it, causing it to be excreted by the body, not absorbed. In comparison, lab rats that ate whole milk had high cholesterol and clogged arteries because the fats did not combine with the calcium and were instead absorbed into the bloodstream.

The probiotics found in fermented foods like cheese and yogurt balance your digestion. Artisanal cheesemakers in the United States are making sensational, unctuous cheeses that you'll love. To get the full benefits of raw cheese, I also recommend you look for cheese made with organic milk from grass-fed cows. Not only is it delicious, but natural, healthy grass-fed milk makes cheese with incredible concentrations of omega-3 fatty acids. An amazing raw cheese and a bottle of Pommard Premier Cru? I'd be a lab rat any day.

FENNEL-ALMOND SOUP, BAY SCALLOPS, FUJI APPLE, AND WATERCRESS

SERVES 4 TO 6

PICKLED APPLES

1 cup apple cider vinegar
1 cup unsweetened apple juice
¼ cup sugar
1 tablespoon pickling spice
1 tablespoon yellow mustard seeds
3 to 4 sprigs fresh thyme
1 bay leaf
1 teaspoon fresh lemon juice
3 Fuji apples

FENNEL-ALMOND PUREE

1 quart whole milk
1 cup slivered blanched almonds
2 fennel bulbs, cored, white part sliced
    (fronds reserved for garnish)
Kosher salt

2 pounds bay scallops
Kosher salt and freshly cracked black pepper
Grapeseed oil
½ cup toasted slivered blanched almonds
1 bunch hydroponic watercress
Extra-virgin olive oil

Pickle the apples. In a medium saucepan, combine the cider vinegar, apple juice, sugar, pickling spice, mustard seeds, thyme, bay leaf, and lemon juice. Bring to a boil and stir until the sugar has dissolved. Remove from the heat and cool a bit. Use a melon baller to make as many balls as possible from the unpeeled apples (each ball will have a little of the pink skin on it). Add the balls to a vacuum-seal bag and then cover with the pickling liquid. Seal on medium pressure and set aside until ready to use.

Make the fennel-almond puree. Pour the milk into a large pot and add the almonds and sliced fennel. Season with salt. Bring to a boil, then reduce the heat and simmer for 25 to 30 minutes, until the almonds and fennel are very tender. When done, carefully pour the entire mixture into a blender and puree until you have a silky, light puree.

Sear the scallops. Pat the scallops dry with paper towels, then season liberally with salt and a little pepper. Heat a large nonstick skillet over high heat. Coat with grapeseed oil and, when hot and shimmering, add the scallops. Sauté for 2 minutes, until the scallops are just cooked through and have some nice color.

To serve, place some toasted almond slivers in the bottom of a shallow bowl. Add a few pickled apple balls, sautéed scallops, and reserved fennel fronds. Add a few sprigs of watercress, then pour some puree into the bowl. Drizzle with a little extra-virgin olive oil.

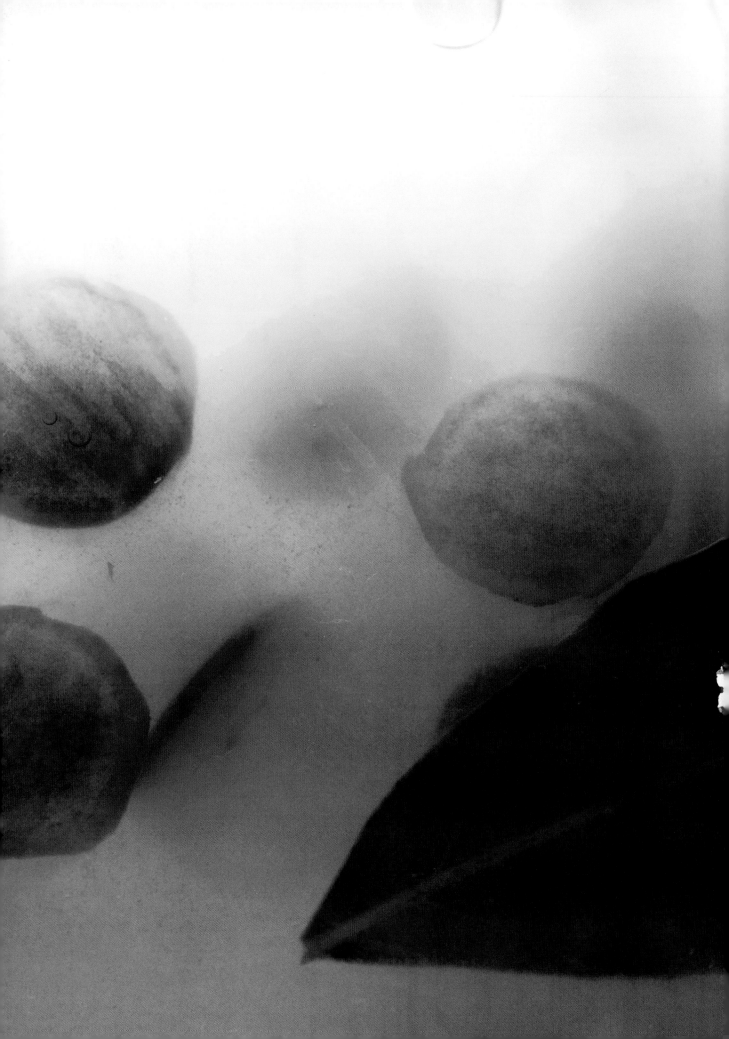

FENNEL WITH SPANISH CHORIZO, CHICKPEAS, PICKLED RHUBARB, AND ORANGE AIOLI

SERVES 4

CHICKPEAS
2 cups dried chickpeas, soaked
   in water overnight
2 or 3 lemon slices
1 teaspoon kosher salt

PICKLED RHUBARB
2 medium rhubarb ribs
½ cup white vinegar
2 tablespoons sugar
2 teaspoons yellow mustard seeds
1 bay leaf
3 or 4 thin slices of shallot
¼ teaspoon kosher salt

BRAISED FENNEL AND CHORIZO
¼ cup extra-virgin olive oil
½ pound cured Spanish chorizo
1 teaspoon ground fennel seeds
1 small fennel bulb, fronds reserved for garnish
Juice of 1 orange
1 cup low-sodium chicken stock
Kosher salt and freshly cracked black pepper

ORANGE AIOLI
2 egg whites
¼ teaspoon Dijon mustard
1 teaspoon fresh lemon juice
2 tablespoons fresh orange juice
1 teaspoon grated orange zest
¼ teaspoon kosher salt
¼ teaspoon sugar
1 cup grapeseed oil

Cook the chickpeas. Drain the chickpeas and place in a medium pot. Add water to cover by 2 inches, the lemon, and salt and bring to a boil over high heat. Reduce the heat to a simmer and cook for 25 to 30 minutes, until the chickpeas are just tender. Drain and set aside.

Pickle the rhubarb. Trim the rhubarb and cut into 3-inch pieces. Using a mandoline, cut the pieces lengthwise into thin slices. Place them in a vacuum-seal bag and set it aside, unsealed. Make a quick pickle solution by combining the vinegar, sugar, mustard seeds, bay leaf, shallots, and salt in a saucepan. Set over high heat and bring to a simmer, about 7 minutes. Once the sugar is dissolved and the mustard seeds are tender, cool slightly. Then pour the solution over the rhubarb strips and seal the bag on medium pressure. Set aside for 15 to 20 minutes.

Cook the fennel and sausage. Set a Dutch oven over low-medium heat and add the olive oil. Cut the chorizo into chunks and pulse in a food processor until the sausage is finely ground. Add to the Dutch oven along with the fennel seeds and cook over low heat for 7 to 8 minutes to infuse the oil and extract the flavors of the sausage. Use a slotted spoon to transfer the chorizo to a plate, and set aside. Trim the fennel bulb and slice into ¼-inch-wide pieces. Add to the chorizo oil and sauté for 2 to 3 minutes, until the fennel is slightly wilted. Add the orange juice and chicken stock, and season with salt and pepper. Return the chorizo to the pot, cover, and braise for 15 minutes, until tender. Fold in the chickpeas and cook for 10 more minutes to bring the flavors together.

Make the aioli. In a blender, combine the egg whites, mustard, lemon juice, orange juice, orange zest, salt, and sugar. Blend until smooth. With the blender running, add the grapeseed oil in a slow, steady stream so the mixture emulsifies. Refrigerate until ready to use.

Serve the chorizo, chickpea, and fennel mixture topped with the pickled rhubarb slices. Garnish with the reserved fennel fronds and the aioli, and drizzle with a little of the chorizo oil from the pot.

quick pickling

In my restaurants, we've been playing around with pickles for a few years now. When done well, traditional pickling methods preserve some of a vegetable's natural crunch and color. However, some hot pickling methods can take up to two weeks and leave the vegetables limp. I don't enjoy them.

Instead, we make quick pickles with vacuum compression, a process you can easily replicate at home using a vacuum sealer as you would to store food. Vacuum compression uses no heat, leaving vegetables and fruits raw, crisp, and dense, with an amazing pickle freshness. Vacuum compression sucks the air out of vegetables and fruits, leaving a very dense, meaty texture that is just sensational. The fruits and vegetables aggressively absorb any liquid that you put into the bag with them. Pickling fresh, sweet onions like shallots is a great way to add a pinpoint amount of savory acid to a dish. Tinker with different recipes. Blueberries pickled with balsamic and cranberry juice. Tomatoes compressed with chili oil and lime. There is no right or wrong. You will become a pickle expert in minutes.

FRESH FIGS WITH FROZEN BASIL CREAM AND BALSAMIC

SERVES 4

BASIL CREAM

2½ cups lightly packed fresh basil leaves
¼ cup extra-virgin olive oil
1 teaspoon fresh lemon juice
1 teaspoon light agave syrup
¼ cup heavy cream

16 fresh California Mission figs
¼ cup fresh basil buds
2 tablespoons good-quality extra-virgin olive oil
3 to 4 tablespoons aged balsamic vinegar
Flaky sea salt
Freshly cracked black pepper

Make the basil cream. Combine all the ingredients in a blender and puree until completely smooth. Pour into a bowl, cover with plastic, and freeze until just set, about 2½ hours; do not overfreeze.

To assemble, slice the figs lengthwise and place cut-side up on plates. Place small scoops of basil cream on and around the figs. Garnish with the basil buds, drizzle with the extra-virgin olive oil and the balsamic, and season with flaky sea salt and freshly cracked black pepper.

PAIN PERDU, ROASTED FIGS, MAPLE, AND ICE CREAM

SERVES 6

VANILLA BEAN ICE CREAM

1½ cups whole milk
1½ cups heavy cream
2 vanilla beans, scraped and split
6 egg yolks
½ cup sugar

ROASTED FIGS

12 large ripe California figs
Extra-virgin olive oil

PAIN PERDU

6 large eggs
1½ cups heavy cream, half-and-half,
    or whole milk
2 tablespoons sugar
¼ teaspoon ground cloves
½ teaspoon ground cinnamon
Pinch ground nutmeg
6 slices (1-inch-thick) brioche bread

4 tablespoons (½ stick) unsalted butter
½ cup crushed toasted almonds
Fresh lemon thyme buds
Confectioners' sugar
½ cup maple syrup

Make the ice cream. Combine the milk and cream in a medium saucepan and set it over medium heat. Add the vanilla beans (both seeds and pods). Bring to a gentle simmer so bubbles form on the surface, then reduce the heat to low. In a large bowl, combine the egg yolks and sugar; whisk together until they turn pale yellow. While whisking, pour about half of the hot milk mixture into the egg mixture. Then pour the egg and milk mixture back into the saucepan and cook over low heat, stirring constantly, until the mixture coats the back of a spoon, about 8 minutes. Set a large bowl over ice and pour the ice cream base through a strainer into the bowl. Discard the vanilla pods and let the ice cream base cool. Once cool, process in an ice cream maker; then place in the freezer to chill.

Roast the figs. Preheat the oven to 400°F. Cut the figs in half lengthwise and place them on a baking sheet, cut side up. Drizzle with the olive oil, and roast in the oven for 10 to 12 minutes, until softened but not mushy.

Make the pain perdu. Turn down the oven temperature to 200°F. Whisk together the eggs, cream, sugar, cloves, cinnamon, and nutmeg in a mixing bowl. Set the slices of bread out in a large rimmed dish, and pour the egg mixture over them. Allow the bread to soak for 5 minutes; then turn the slices over and allow to soak for 5 more minutes.

In a large nonstick sauté pan, heat 1 tablespoon of the butter over medium heat. Add a batch of bread slices, and cook for 2 to 3 minutes per side, until deep golden brown. Keep warm in the oven while you cook the rest, adding 1 tablespoon butter to the pan for each batch.

To assemble, serve the pain perdu topped with the roasted figs and a quenelle of vanilla ice cream. Garnish with crushed almonds, lemon thyme buds, and confectioners' sugar, and drizzle with maple syrup.

KALE SALAD WITH APPLE, WALNUTS, AND ROASTED GRAPE VINAIGRETTE

SERVES 4

VINAIGRETTE

½ pound red seedless California grapes
2 tablespoons honey
¼ cup extra-virgin olive oil, plus more
    for drizzling
Kosher salt and freshly cracked black pepper
2 tablespoons apple cider vinegar
Squeeze of fresh lemon juice

2 Golden Delicious apples
Extra-virgin olive oil
Kosher salt and freshly cracked black pepper
1 cup walnut halves
4 cups lightly packed mixed winter green leaves
    (such as green and purple kale, beet greens,
    and chard)
½ cup crumbled mild blue cheese,
    such as Humboldt Fog

Make the vinaigrette. Preheat the oven to 450°F. Cut the grapes into small clusters, reserving a handful of loose grapes. In a large cast-iron pan, combine the grape clusters, honey, and a drizzle of olive oil. Season with salt. Toss to coat evenly, then roast in the oven for 10 to 12 minutes, until the grape skins are slightly blistered. Remove from the oven and carefully transfer the roasted grape clusters to a plate and set aside. Allow the pan to cool slightly, then add the cider vinegar, lemon juice, and ¼ cup olive oil. Season with a little pepper, then add the reserved raw grapes to the pan. Use a whisk to crush the grapes and mix the liquid into a vinaigrette.

Roast the apples and walnuts. Core the apples and slice them horizontally into ¼-inch-thick slices. Arrange them on a baking sheet, drizzle with olive oil, and season with salt and pepper. Arrange the walnuts in a single layer on a small roasting tray. Roast the apples and walnuts for 15 to 17 minutes, until the apples are slightly puffy and the walnuts are deeply colored. Remove, and season the walnuts with salt while still hot.

Prepare the kale. Wash the greens, then remove any tough stems so you have only the tender leaves. Tear into bite-size pieces if needed.

To serve, set the apple slices on a large platter and top with small clusters of roasted grapes. Scatter with the greens. Crumble the blue cheese and walnuts over the top. Drizzle with the roasted grape vinaigrette, and serve.

SONOMA LAMB WITH APRICOT MUSTARD, CURRY, CHICKPEAS, AND LETTUCE

SERVES 2 TO 3

CHICKPEAS
2 cups dried black chickpeas, soaked
    overnight in water to cover
1 bay leaf
2 lemon slices
1 teaspoon kosher salt

CURRY MAYO
2 egg whites
1 tablespoon curry powder
½ teaspoon Dijon mustard
2 teaspoons fresh lemon juice
¼ teaspoon kosher salt
¼ teaspoon sugar
1 cup grapeseed oil

PICKLED SHALLOTS
1 cup white wine vinegar
¼ cup sugar
½ teaspoon kosher salt
2 shallots

APRICOTS
6 fresh apricots, halved and pitted
2 tablespoons sugar
Juice of ½ lemon
1 tablespoon whole-grain mustard
1 tablespoon Dijon mustard

LAMB
1 whole rack of lamb (about 8 ribs,
    1½ pounds total), frenched
Grapeseed oil
Kosher salt and freshly cracked black pepper

Butter lettuce leaves
Nasturtium leaves
Flowering cilantro

Cook the chickpeas. Drain the chickpeas, then add to a large pot along with 9 cups of water and the bay leaf, lemon, and salt. Bring to a boil over high heat. Then reduce the heat and simmer for 1 hour, until tender. Drain the chickpeas and keep warm.

Make the curry mayo. In a blender, combine the egg whites, curry powder, mustard, lemon juice, salt, and sugar. With the blender running, add the grapeseed oil in a slow, steady stream so the mixture emulsifies. Refrigerate until ready to serve.

Pickle the shallots. Combine the vinegar, sugar, salt, and ½ cup of water in a small saucepan. Heat and stir until the sugar has dissolved, then allow to cool. Slice the shallots and place them in a vacuum-seal bag; add the pickling liquid. Compress on the highest pressure setting, then refrigerate for at least 1 hour before using.

Prepare the apricots. Place the apricot halves in a vacuum-seal bag. Dissolve the sugar in 2 tablespoons of hot water. Add the lemon juice, and then pour the mixture into the bag and seal on medium pressure. Open the bag and drain the apricots. Transfer 4 apricot halves to a food processor, and add some of the pickling liquid and both mustards. Process until well combined. Set the apricot mustard and the remaining apricot halves aside until ready to serve.

Cook the lamb. Preheat the oven to 375°F. Heat an ovenproof skillet over high heat. Rub the lamb rack all over with grapeseed oil and season with salt and pepper. Sear fat-side down for 5 to 7 minutes, until well browned. Turn the rack fat-side up and place the pan in the the oven. Roast for 10 to 15 minutes, until medium rare (the internal temperature should reach about 135°F). Then remove from the oven and let rest for 5 to 10 minutes before slicing into thick chops.

Serve the rack of lamb slathered with the curry mayo and topped with the black chickpeas, pickled shallots, and pressed apricots. Garnish with butter lettuce, nasturtium leaves, and cilantro, and serve with the apricot mustard.

roasting/searing

Understanding the techniques of roasting and searing is the cornerstone of being a great cook. What gives meat its flavor is a caramelization process known as the Maillard reaction, during which the amino acids in protein melt and bond with the naturally present sugars. This happens between 300° and 500°F. The result is a rich crust, a roasted aroma, and an incredible, deep flavor.

Starting off with the right cut for the job is the first step in maximizing the flavor of meat. A steak needs to be thick, with enough marbling that it doesn't dry out in the pan.

The next important factor is surface moisture. Damp or wet meat will steam before the caramelization process starts. Allowing the meat to come to room temperature will prevent sweating, which also slows down the Maillard process.

The next step is the sear. Season only with salt at first; pepper will burn. Get your pan scorching, screaming hot. Add an ample amount of oil, depending on how much you're cooking, then carefully lay your cut in the pan away from you, not toward you.

Turning cuts frequently will speed up the browning process as the surface not touching the pan won't have as much time to cool. If it's a 2-inch steak, don't cut into it; an instant-read digital thermometer will give you an exact reading of what's going on inside: 125°F for rare, 130° to 135°F for medium rare, 140°F for medium, and so on.

If you are roasting larger pieces like a bone-in rib eye or rack of lamb, transfer the entire pan (assuming your pan is all-metal construction) with your gorgeous brown cut to a preheated 325°F oven. This minimizes shrinkage and provides the most flavorful, juicy, and tender results. Keep the oven door closed. Roast. Smell. Smile.

When your meat is done, resting is a very important step. Meat is nearly 75 percent water. Roasting and searing constricts the proteins, which forces moisture out of the cells. Resting the fibers allows moisture to be held inside. Slice and finish with coarse sea salt and freshly cracked pepper.

SCALLOPS WITH MELON, CHILE, AND MINT

PRESSED MELON

¼ cup sugar
Grated zest and juice of 1 lime
½ cantaloupe (about ¾ pound)
½ honeydew melon (about ¾ pound)
½ red seedless watermelon (about ¾ pound)

24 fresh bay scallops
2½ cups 1-inch cubes of cantaloupe
2 tablespoons fresh lime juice
1 tablespoon fresh orange juice
1 serrano chile, finely sliced
¼ cup grapeseed oil
¼ teaspoon finely grated lime zest
2 teaspoons fresh mint leaves and buds
Flaky sea salt

Compress the melon. Combine the sugar, ¼ cup of water, and the lime zest and juice in a bowl and stir until the sugar has completely dissolved. Using a melon baller, scoop out small balls of cantaloupe, honeydew, and watermelon. Place them in a vacuum-seal bag, add the lime syrup, and seal on medium pressure. It is ready to use straightaway, but you can store it in the fridge until ready to use.

Prepare the scallops. Remove the tough outer muscle from each scallop and discard it. Using a sharp knife, cut each scallop in half horizontally. Arrange the sliced scallops on a chilled plate. Keep cold until ready to serve.

Make the marinade. In a blender, combine the cantaloupe cubes with the lime juice, orange juice, and a little of the chile. Blend until completely smooth. With the blender running, slowly drizzle in the grapeseed oil to emulsify the puree. Spoon the cantaloupe sauce over the scallop slices and marinate for 7 to 8 minutes.

Arrange the pressed melon balls on top of the scallops. Garnish with the grated lime zest, some more sliced chile, and the mint. Season with a little flaky sea salt.

PRESSED WATERMELON WITH BLOOD ORANGE SORBET, GOAT CHEESE, BLACK OLIVE, AND BASIL

SERVES 2 TO 4

BLOOD ORANGE SORBET
¾ cup sugar
1 tablespoon grated orange zest
4 cups fresh blood orange juice
¼ cup fresh lemon juice

¼ ripe seedless watermelon, halved lengthwise, then crosswise
1 orange
½ cup crumbled goat cheese
½ cup pitted black olives, such as Kalamata
2 tablespoons fresh purple basil buds
Micro basil
Extra-virgin olive oil
Flaky sea salt

Make the sorbet. Combine 1 cup of water with the sugar and orange zest in a saucepan and bring to a simmer. Stir until the sugar dissolves, about 7 minutes. Remove from the heat and add the blood orange juice and lemon juice. Allow the liquid to cool, then transfer it to an ice cream maker. Freeze according to the instructions to create the sorbet, about 20 minutes (depending on the machine). Place in a resealable container and store in the freezer for 1 hour to firm up before using.

Compress the watermelon. Cut the watermelon into ½- to ¾-inch-thick half-moon slices. Place in a vacuum-seal bag and seal on the highest pressure setting. This technique removes the air from the watermelon, giving it a very dense, meaty texture. Refrigerate for 10 minutes or until ready to serve.

Use a sharp knife to slice off the rind and pith from the orange. Cut between the membranes to free the orange segments.

Serve the pressed watermelon slices topped with the crumbled goat cheese, black olives, orange supremes, purple basil, and micro basil. Add quenelles of the orange sorbet, a drizzle of olive oil, and some sea salt.

SEARED HALIBUT WITH CRUSHED WATERMELON GAZPACHO AND LIME

SERVES 4

WATERMELON GAZPACHO

2 cups cubed watermelon
4 heirloom tomatoes (assorted colors), diced
4 or 5 radishes
2 avocados
¼ serrano chile, seeded and diced
Kosher salt and freshly cracked black pepper
1 teaspoon sugar
Juice of 1 lime
¼ cup extra-virgin olive oil

HALIBUT

2 tablespoons grapeseed oil
4 (6-ounce) boneless, skinless halibut fillets
Kosher salt and freshly cracked black pepper
1 tablespoon unsalted butter
2 sprigs fresh thyme

1 lime
Fresh cilantro sprigs
Flaky sea salt

Prepare the watermelon gazpacho. Use a mortar and pestle to roughly crush the watermelon. Drain any juices into a bowl and transfer the crushed watermelon to a second large bowl. Repeat the process with the tomatoes, radishes, avocados, and chile, crushing each separately so the colors and flavors remain separate and adding any juices to the first bowl. Gently fold the crushed ingredients together.

Season the reserved juices with salt, pepper, and the sugar. Add the lime juice, then drizzle in the olive oil while whisking to lightly emulsify. Set the vinaigrette aside until ready to serve.

Cook the fish. Preheat the oven to 350°F. Heat a large ovenproof sauté pan over high heat and add the grapeseed oil. Pat the fish dry with paper towels, and season well on both sides with salt and pepper. Place the fish in the hot pan and cook without moving the fish for 2 minutes, or until you can see it getting nice and golden. Add the butter and thyme to the pan, and baste the fish with the melted butter. Place the pan in the oven and cook for 3 to 4 minutes.

Use a sharp knife to slice off the rind and pith from the lime. Cut between the membranes to free the lime segments.

To serve, spoon some gazpacho onto each plate. Top with the lime segments. Dress lightly with the vinaigrette and top with a piece of seared halibut. Garnish with cilantro sprigs and season with flaky sea salt.

POACHED SHRIMP, SWEET PICKLED WATERMELON, GREEN GODDESS, AND RADISH SPROUTS

SERVES 4

WATERMELON PICKLES
1 cup champagne vinegar
¼ cup sugar
¼ teaspoon kosher salt
½ lemon, sliced
½ small red seedless watermelon

SHRIMP
1 lemon, cut in half
Kosher salt
16 medium shrimp, shelled and deveined

GREEN GODDESS DRESSING
1 oil-packed anchovy fillet
¼ teaspoon Dijon mustard
½ teaspoon grated lemon zest
1 tablespoon fresh lemon juice
½ teaspoon sugar
¾ cup grapeseed oil
Kosher salt and freshly cracked black pepper
2 tablespoons flat-leaf parsley
2 tablespoons chopped fresh tarragon
2 tablespoons chopped fresh chives
½ avocado, pitted, peeled, and cubed

1 avocado, pitted, peeled, and cut into
   thin crescents
Radish sprouts

Make the watermelon pickles. In a large pot, combine the vinegar, sugar, salt, and lemon with 1 cup of water. Bring to a boil and stir until the sugar has completely dissolved. Remove from the heat and cool completely. Using a sharp knife, slice off the thin layer of green skin from the watermelon, leaving the rind. Cut the watermelon into ½-inch-thick rounds. Cut the rind into wedges and the red flesh into ½-inch cubes. Place the watermelon cubes and rinds in a vacuum-seal bag. Cover with the cooled brine and seal on medium pressure. Once it is completely sealed, remove from the bag, drain off the brine, and set the pickle aside until ready to serve.

Poach the shrimp. Set a medium pot of water over high heat and add the lemon and salt. Bring to a simmer and add the shrimp. Return the water to a simmer, then remove from the heat and let the residual heat cook the shrimp. When they are completely pink, after about 5 minutes, strain the shrimp and set aside to cool. Refrigerate until ready to use.

Make the Green Goddess dressing. In a blender, combine the anchovy, mustard, lemon zest and juice, and sugar. With the blender running, slowly drizzle in the grapeseed oil until the dressing emulsifies. Season with salt and pepper. Add the parsley, tarragon, chives, and avocado and blend until completely smooth. Add water to thin if the dressing seems too thick.

Dot the plate with the Green Goddess, and top with the poached shrimp and pickled watermelon cubes and rinds. Garnish with the avocado crescents and radish sprouts.

OCTOPUS WITH AIOLI, LEMON CRUSHED POTATOES, AND FRIED CAPERS

SERVES 6 TO 8

OCTOPUS

1 medium fresh octopus (3 to 4 pounds)
1 carrot, cut in half
3 celery ribs
½ fennel bulb, sliced
1 onion, cut in half
1 head garlic, split through the equator
5 or 6 sprigs fresh flat-leaf parsley
6 sprigs fresh thyme
3 bay leaves
3 or 4 black peppercorns
1 teaspoon kosher salt

LEMON CRUSHED POTATOES

1½ pounds medium Yukon Gold potatoes
½ lemon
2 garlic cloves
4 sprigs fresh thyme, leaves only
Kosher salt and freshly cracked black pepper
1 teaspoon grated lemon zest
Extra-virgin olive oil

CHILE OIL

3 tablespoons dried red pepper flakes
¾ cup grapeseed oil
2 garlic cloves
2 or 3 sprigs fresh thyme
Kosher salt

AIOLI

2 egg whites
1 garlic clove, minced
2 teaspoons fresh lemon juice
½ teaspoon Dijon mustard
¼ teaspoon kosher salt
¼ teaspoon sugar
1 cup grapeseed oil

Extra-virgin olive oil, for frying
2 to 3 tablespoons salt-packed capers, rinsed
   and drained
3 tablespoons micro arugula

Make the octopus. Remove the head from the octopus and discard the beak and tough cartilage. Slice the head into long fat strips so they are about the same thickness as the tentacles (this will ensure that everything cooks evenly). Separate the tentacles into individual pieces. Place the octopus in a large stockpot and cover with cold water. Add the carrot, celery, fennel, onion, garlic, parsley, thyme, bay leaves, and peppercorns. Season with the salt. Bring to a boil over high heat. Once boiling, reduce the heat, cover the pot, and simmer gently for approximately 2 hours, or until the octopus is tender. Allow to cool in the liquid.

Make the potatoes. Place the potatoes in a pan of cold water with the lemon, garlic, and thyme. Season with salt and bring to a boil. Cook for 45 to 50 minutes, until the potatoes are tender. Drain, discard the aromatics, and gently break the potatoes up with a potato masher. Fold in the lemon zest, season with salt and pepper, and finish with a drizzle of olive oil.

Make the chile oil. Combine the red pepper flakes, grapeseed oil, garlic, and thyme in a saucepan. Warm over low-medium heat for 15 to 20 minutes to infuse the oil. Season with salt. Allow to cool, then discard the garlic and thyme.

Make the aioli. In a blender, blend the egg whites until just foamy, about 10 seconds. Add the garlic, lemon juice, mustard, salt, and sugar. With the blender running, add the grapeseed oil in a slow, steady stream so the mixture emulsifies. Refrigerate until ready to use.

Fry the capers. Fill a sauté pan with ¼ inch of olive oil, set it over medium-high heat, and heat the oil to 350°F. Rinse the capers and pat dry. Fry, in batches, for 1 to 2 minutes, until golden and slightly bursting. Drain on paper towels.

Drain the octopus and use a sharp knife to slice it very thin. Serve with the lemon crushed potatoes, fried capers, aioli, and chile oil. Garnish with the micro arugula.

octopus

Never considered serving octopus for dinner before? Why not? It's delicious. Octopus is one of the most environmentally friendly deep-sea catches, cherished in both Mediterranean and Japanese cuisine. Loaded with vitamin B_{12}, and essential omega-3 fatty acids, octopus contains only 140 calories for a 3.5-ounce serving. The nutrients in octopus have been shown to be effective in reducing the risk of heart disease, cancer, and depression.

Environmentally, octopus is considered a good choice to supplement your seafood consumption because of its very efficient life cycle and quick reproduction rate. An octopus lives for only about a year and is ready to reproduce at around six months. Compared with tuna, which is at the top of the trophic scale and can live for fifteen years or more, and lobster, which is near the bottom of the trophic scale and averages seven years of growth for every pound of weight, octopus provides more nutrients and consumes fewer resources over a shorter period of time. Because octopus is harvested by simple fishing practices (basically a bucket and a rope), eating it is practically environmentally neutral in terms of the impact on its natural habitat.

CHARRED CALAMARI, BACON AIOLI, BLACK-EYED PEAS, AND PIPÉRADE

SERVES 4

BLACK-EYED PEAS
1½ cups dried black-eyed peas
2 lemon slices
Kosher salt
2 bay leaves

PIPÉRADE
1 medium yellow onion
2 celery ribs
1 fennel bulb, cored
4 vine-ripened tomatoes
1 red bell pepper
2 garlic cloves
1 fresh red chile
1 bay leaf
2 tablespoons extra-virgin olive oil
Kosher salt and freshly cracked black pepper

BACON AIOLI
4 strips thick-cut bacon
¾ cup plus 1 teaspoon grapeseed oil
2 egg whites
¼ teaspoon minced garlic
¼ teaspoon Dijon mustard
½ teaspoon grated lemon zest
1 tablespoon fresh lemon juice
½ teaspoon sugar
Kosher salt and freshly cracked black pepper

2 garlic cloves, minced
2 sprigs fresh thyme, leaves picked
Pinch red pepper flakes
1 teaspoon red wine vinegar
Kosher salt and freshly cracked black pepper

GARLIC CHIPS
1 cup extra-virgin olive oil
4 garlic cloves, finely sliced lengthwise
    on a mandoline
Flaky sea salt

CALAMARI
1½ pounds cleaned calamari, tentacles
    separated from bodies
1 tablespoon grapeseed oil
Flaky sea salt and freshly cracked black pepper
1 lemon, halved

Fresh fennel fronds
Fresh thyme leaves

Cook the black-eyed peas. Rinse the black-eyed peas under cold running water. Drain, place in a large pot, and add enough water to cover the peas by 2 inches. Add the lemon slices, salt, and bay leaves, and bring to a simmer. Cover and cook for 45 to 60 minutes, until the peas are tender. Drain and set aside.

Make the pipérade. Preheat the oven to 375°F. Slice the onion, celery, and fennel bulb. Roughly chop the tomatoes. Seed and slice the bell pepper. Arrange the vegetables in a roasting pan with the garlic, chile, and bay leaf. Drizzle with the olive oil and season with salt and pepper. Roast for 40 to 45 minutes, until soft. Discard the bay leaf, transfer the vegetables to a food processor, and pulse 3 or 4 times.

Make the bacon aioli. Slice the strips of bacon on the bias to yield 1½-inch-long lardons. Set a large sauté pan over medium-high heat. Add the lardons and the teaspoon of grapeseed oil and cook while stirring so they curl up as they crisp. Cook until crispy and golden, about 8 minutes. Drain on paper towels. Pour half the fat from the pan into a blender (reserve the rest in the pan) and add the egg whites, garlic, mustard, lemon zest, lemon juice, and sugar. With the blender running, slowly drizzle in the ¾ cup grapeseed oil until the aioli is thick and emulsified. Taste the aioli and season with salt and pepper.

Return the bacon pan to medium heat. Add the garlic, thyme, and red pepper flakes to the remaining fat in the pan. Let it sizzle and infuse the oil. Add the black-eyed peas. Add the vinegar and season with salt and pepper. Toss well to coat and warm through.

Make the garlic chips. Place the olive oil and garlic slices in a small sauté pan and set over low heat. Cook slowly until the garlic sizzles and becomes golden brown and crisp, 2 to 3 minutes. Use a slotted spoon to transfer the garlic chips to a paper towel to drain. Season with salt. Reserve the garlic oil.

Make the calamari. Pat the calamari dry with paper towels, then drizzle with the grapeseed oil and season with salt and pepper. Set a large sauté pan over high heat. When the pan is extremely hot, add the calamari and cook without moving for 1 minute so it gets a nice sear on it. Turn the calamari and sear the other side for 1 more minute. Add a squeeze of fresh lemon juice to the pan and stir. Remove from the heat.

To assemble, spread 1 heaping tablespoon of pipérade on each plate. Top with charred calamari and scatter with black-eyed peas. Garnish with the reserved fennel fronds, thyme leaves, and crispy garlic chips. Dot with the bacon aioli. Drizzle with a little of the reserved garlic oil.

PORK BELLY WITH SWEET ONION PICKLES, BANANA MUSTARD, AND THYME

SERVES 4

PORK BELLY

1 (3-pound) piece of pork belly, skin removed
Extra-virgin olive oil
Kosher salt and freshly cracked black pepper
1 large carrot, roughly chopped
2 celery ribs, roughly chopped
1 medium onion, roughly chopped
2 garlic cloves, sliced
1 bay leaf
6 sprigs fresh thyme
2 cups chicken stock

BANANA CHIPS

1 green banana
Extra-virgin olive oil

ONION PICKLES

1 large Vidalia onion
1 tablespoon apple cider vinegar
1 tablespoon sugar
Kosher salt and freshly cracked black pepper
Extra-virgin olive oil

BANANA MUSTARD

2 firm but ripe bananas
3 tablespoons whole-grain mustard

Grapeseed oil
Extra-virgin olive oil
Fresh thyme buds

Make the pork belly. Portion the pork belly into 2 strips. Set a Dutch oven over high heat and add a drizzle of olive oil. Season the pork belly pieces well with salt and pepper. Sear for 3 to 4 minutes on each side so they get some good color all over. Remove from the pan and set aside. Add the carrot, celery, onion, garlic, bay leaf, and thyme to the Dutch oven and sauté until the vegetables are lightly colored and fragrant, 5 to 7 minutes. Add the chicken stock and stir—this will be the marinade. Remove from the heat and allow to cool to lukewarm. Place each strip of pork in a vacuum-seal bag and add the vegetables and braising liquid. Seal on the highest pressure. Then place the bags in a water bath at 190°F. Cook at a steady, consistent temperature for 5 hours. (See page 33 for more on sous vide cooking.) When done, transfer the bags to a bowl of ice water to stop the cooking process. Remove from the ice water and place flat in the fridge to chill.

Make the banana chips and onion pickles. Preheat the oven to 300°F. Peel the green banana and thinly slice it lengthwise on a mandoline. Drizzle with a little olive oil and arrange in a single layer on a parchment-lined baking sheet. Bake for 25 to 30 minutes, until crispy and wafer-like. Slice the onion into ¼-inch-thick rings and place in a bowl, mix together the vinegar and sugar, and toss with the onions. Season with salt and pepper. Place in a single layer on a roasting tray and drizzle with olive oil. Bake for 25 minutes, until the onions are falling apart. Finish under the broiler for 1 minute to brown them.

Make the banana mustard. Preheat the oven to 350°F. Roast the bananas in their skins for 30 minutes. Then discard the skins and puree the banana flesh with the whole-grain mustard in a food processor until smooth.

When ready to serve, remove the pork belly strips from the bags, dry on paper towels, and portion into 4 equal pieces. Trim the edges so they are straight. In a very hot sauté pan, heat a drizzle of grapeseed oil. Sear the pork pieces all over to crisp.

Serve the seared pork belly with the banana mustard, sweet pickled onions, and banana chips. Drizzle with a little extra-virgin olive oil and garnish with thyme buds.

PORK SHOULDER, MUSHROOMS, BARLEY, POACHED EGG, AND HOT SAUCE

SERVES 4 TO 6

The roasted mushrooms and stock can be made a day or two ahead of time.

ROASTED MUSHROOMS AND MUSHROOM STOCK

2 pounds assorted wild mushrooms
   (cremini, shiitake, oyster, cèpe)
2 tablespoons canola oil
2 tablespoons soy sauce
Kosher salt and freshly cracked black pepper
½ cup dry sherry
1 onion, quartered
4 garlic cloves, smashed
1 (2-inch) piece fresh ginger, smashed
1 quart low-sodium chicken stock
2 tablespoons white miso

PORK SHOULDER

1 boneless pork shoulder (3 pounds)
¼ cup soy sauce
1 tablespoon honey
Kosher salt and freshly cracked black pepper

MUSHROOM-BARLEY RISOTTO

1 cup pearl barley
1 teaspoon kosher salt, plus extra for sprinkling
Juice of ½ lemon
2 tablespoons chopped scallions, white and
   green parts

4 to 6 eggs
Hot sauce, such as Sriracha
¼ cup finely sliced scallions, green part only,
   soaked in ice water
2 teaspoons toasted sesame seeds

Prepare the mushrooms and stock. Preheat the oven to 400°F. Clean and quarter the mushrooms. Place them on a rimmed baking sheet, drizzle with the canola oil and soy sauce, and season with salt and pepper. Roast for 20 to 25 minutes, until well caramelized and deeply colored. Remove from the oven and transfer half of the roasted mushrooms to a platter; set aside to use in the barley. Set the baking sheet over a burner on high heat and deglaze the sheet with the sherry, using a wooden spoon to scrape up all the bits. Transfer the mushrooms and liquid to a large pot, and add the onion, garlic, ginger, chicken stock, and miso. Simmer for 45 minutes. Strain the stock, discarding the solids, and keep warm.

Roast the pork. Reduce the oven temperature to 275°F. Rub the pork shoulder all over with the soy sauce and honey, and place in a roasting pan. Season with salt and pepper. Roast for 3 hours.

Make the risotto. Place the barley in a large saucepan and cover with 3 cups of water. Add the salt and lemon juice. Simmer for 35 to 40 minutes, until the barley is tender and the liquid is just about completely absorbed. Fold in the reserved roasted mushrooms. Season with salt and sprinkle with the chopped scallions.

Soft poach the eggs. Preheat a sous vide water bath to 143.5°F. Place the eggs in the bath and cook for 50 minutes. When done, remove from the water, and when cool enough to handle, carefully remove the top half of each shell. Gently slide out an egg onto each plate.

Slice the pork and serve it with the eggs on the mushroom-barley risotto. Top with some hot sauce. Ladle the mushroom stock over, and top with a generous amount of finely sliced scallion greens and a sprinkle of toasted sesame seeds.

HERB-ROASTED PORK LOIN WITH BANANAS, CHARRED ONION, AND HERB AIOLI

SERVES 4 TO 6

PORK

1 (2-pound) boneless pork loin roast, tied
2 garlic cloves
1 tablespoon chopped fresh rosemary leaves,
   plus 4 whole sprigs
1 tablespoon chopped fresh sage leaves,
   plus 4 whole sprigs
1 tablespoon chopped fresh thyme leaves,
   plus 6 whole sprigs
Kosher salt and freshly cracked black pepper
¼ cup extra-virgin olive oil
2 slightly unripe yellow bananas, peeled and
   cut on the bias into ½-inch-thick pieces
1 medium sweet onion, such as Vidalia,
   peeled and sliced into ¼-inch-thick rounds

HERB AIOLI

2 teaspoons chopped fresh rosemary leaves
2 teaspoons chopped fresh sage leaves
2 teaspoons chopped fresh thyme leaves
¼ cup flat-leaf parsley leaves
2 egg whites
½ teaspoon Dijon mustard
1 teaspoon fresh lemon juice
Kosher salt
¾ cup grapeseed oil

Prepare the pork. Preheat the oven to 375°F. Set the pork roast on the counter for 30 minutes to come to room temperature.

Using a mortar and pestle, crush the garlic, chopped herb leaves (do not use the stems), and salt and pepper until everything is well combined, then add the olive oil and continue to crush to form a paste. Rub the paste all over the pork loin. Set the pork loin on a wire rack over a roasting tray and place the extra whole sprigs of rosemary, sage, and thyme directly in the pan under the rack. Roast in the center of the oven for 1 hour 20 minutes in total. After 50 minutes add the banana pieces and sliced onion to the pan. Return to the oven and roast 30 minutes longer, until the internal temperature reaches 140°F and the bananas and onion are well caramelized. Set the pork aside on a platter to rest before carving into slices. Toss the bananas and onion in the pan juices to coat evenly.

Prepare the herb aioli. In a blender combine all the ingredients except the grapeseed oil and blend until smooth. With the blender running, slowly drizzle in the oil until the mixture emulsifies. Thin with a little water if desired.

Serve the sliced pork with the bananas, onion, and herbs from the roasting pan. Drizzle with the pan drippings, and dot with the herb aioli.

POTATO CHIPS WITH FRENCH ONION DIP AND CAVIAR

SERVES 6 TO 8

ONION DIP

2 tablespoons extra-virgin olive oil
2 large yellow onions, sliced
Kosher salt and freshly cracked black pepper
1 teaspoon garlic powder
2 teaspoons onion powder
¾ cup sour cream
¾ cup mayonnaise
⅓ cup cream cheese, at room temperature
3 teaspoons fresh lemon juice

POTATO CHIPS

1 pound medium Yukon Gold potatoes
Canola oil, for deep frying
Flaky sea salt

1 ounce sturgeon caviar
1 ounce paddlefish roe
1 ounce salmon roe
1 tablespoon fresh chervil leaves
1 tablespoon sliced fresh chives
2 teaspoons fresh tarragon leaves
1 teaspoon fresh marjoram buds
2 teaspoons chopped flat-leaf parsley

Make the dip. Set a large sauté pan over medium-high heat. Add the olive oil and onions, and season with salt, pepper, the garlic powder, and the onion powder. Cook while stirring for 20 to 25 minutes, until the onions turn a deep color and are just about falling apart. Set aside to cool completely. In a large mixing bowl combine the sour cream, mayonnaise, cream cheese, and lemon juice. Mix in the cooled caramelized onions. Taste and season with salt if required.

Fry the potato chips. Wash and lightly scrub the potatoes under cold running water. Using a mandoline or a sharp knife, cut the potatoes into ⅛-inch-thick slices and drop into a bowl of cold water—this will prevent them from turning brown and also remove any excess starch. Drain the potato slices and squeeze dry in a kitchen towel. Fill a large pot about two-thirds full with canola oil and heat to 350°F. Fry the chips, in batches, for 2 to 3 minutes, occasionally stirring gently as they fry. When golden brown and crispy, remove with a strainer and drain well. Set on paper towels and season immediately with salt. Bring the oil back up to temperature and continue cooking the chips in batches until all the potatoes are fried.

To serve, top the onion dip with the sturgeon caviar, and paddlefish and salmon roe. Garnish with the fresh herbs. Serve with crispy Yukon chips.

ALASKAN HALIBUT WITH CRISPY POTATO AND ROOT CHIPS

SERVES 4

LEMON AIOLI
2 egg whites
¼ teaspoon Dijon mustard
2 tablespoons fresh lemon juice
½ teaspoon grated lemon zest
¼ teaspoon kosher salt
¼ teaspoon sugar
1 cup grapeseed oil

CHIPS
Canola oil, for deep frying
2 small purple potatoes
2 medium Yukon Gold potatoes
2 small yellow beets
2 small red beets
2 organic carrots
2 parsnips
Kosher salt

FISH
1½ pounds boneless, skinless halibut fillets
Canola oil, for deep frying
2¼ cups all-purpose flour, plus extra for dredging
¾ cup cornstarch
1½ teaspoons kosher salt, plus extra
    for sprinkling
1½ cups ice-cold club soda

Micro basil

Make the lemon aioli. In a blender, combine the egg whites, mustard, lemon juice, lemon zest, salt, and sugar. Blend until combined. With the blender running, add the grapeseed oil in a slow, steady stream so the mixture emulsifies.

Make the chips. In a large pot, heat 3 to 4 inches of canola oil to 280°F. Peel each of the vegetables and thinly slice on a mandoline or with a sharp knife. Place the slices in separate bowls of ice water (so the colors don't run together). Rinse the vegetables in cold water until the water is no longer cloudy; this removes the excess starch and helps the vegetables crisp up when fried. Drain and dry the vegetable chips. Fry the chips separately in small batches in the hot oil for 6 to 8 minutes, until they are crisped but not browned. Remove with a slotted spoon and drain on paper towels.

Make the fish. Cut the halibut into smaller (3- to 4-ounce) portions. Add canola oil to the same pot the vegetables were fried in if needed to reach three-quarters full, and heat it to 375°F. In a large mixing bowl, combine the flour, cornstarch, and salt. Make a well in the center and gradually pour in the club soda, whisking constantly. Working your way from the center out, slowly incorporate the dry ingredients to form a smooth, light batter. Lightly dredge the fish pieces in flour, then dip in the batter. Carefully drop into the hot oil and fry for 6 to 7 minutes, until crispy and golden brown, turning to brown on both sides. Drain on paper towels, then season with salt while hot.

Return the oil to 375°F and add the par-fried chips, in batches, cooking for 1 to 2 minutes to crisp up. The second frying gives the chips a really nice crisp. Drain, and season with salt.

Serve the crispy fish with the root vegetable chips and dot with the lemon aioli. Garnish with micro basil and season with more salt.

SMOKED TROUT, VODKA CRÈME FRAÎCHE, AND CRISPY POTATOES

MAKES 20 TO 25 PIECES

POTATOES

1½ pounds baby creamer potatoes
   in assorted colors
Extra-virgin olive oil
Kosher salt
Canola oil, for deep frying

VODKA CRÈME FRAÎCHE

1 cup crème fraîche
2 tablespoons vodka
Kosher salt

FRIED SHALLOTS

1 shallot, thinly sliced
½ cup all-purpose flour
Olive oil, for shallow frying
Kosher salt

8 to 10 ounces smoked trout, bones removed
   and flaked in bite-size pieces
Radish sprouts
Chopped fresh chives
Fleur de sel
Extra-virgin olive oil

Cook the potatoes. Preheat the oven to 350°F. Place the potatoes in a roasting pan and drizzle with olive oil. Season with salt and stir to evenly coat the potatoes. Roast for 30 to 35 minutes, until the potatoes are soft. Remove from the oven and allow to cool slightly. While the potatoes are still warm, gently press down on each one with the back of a pan or the side of a knife, so it flattens to about ¾ inch but stays intact (it's okay if the edges crack a bit, as they will get extra-crisp when fried).

Heat about 4 inches of canola oil in a heavy pot over medium heat. Once the oil reaches 350°F, fry the crushed potatoes, in batches, for 5 to 6 minutes, until they become golden and crunchy. Drain on paper towels and season with salt.

Make the vodka crème fraîche. Combine the crème fraîche and vodka in a mixing bowl and whisk vigorously to whip and combine. Season lightly with salt. Refrigerate until ready to use.

Fry the shallots. Separate the shallot slices into rings. Lightly dredge the rings in the flour. In a sauté pan, heat ½ inch of olive oil to 350°F. Fry the shallots for 2 to 3 minutes, until golden brown. Drain on paper towels and immediately season with salt.

To assemble, place a small dollop of vodka crème fraîche on each piece of potato and top it with a piece of trout. Garnish with the radish sprouts, chives, and fried shallots. Season with fleur de sel and drizzle with a little olive oil.

POTATO PATCH

SERVES 4 TO 6

BEET "SOIL"
3 to 4 medium beets
¼ cup shelled pistachios, toasted
Kosher salt and freshly cracked black pepper
2 to 3 teaspoons extra-virgin olive oil

POTATO DUMPLINGS
2 pounds large Russet potatoes
Extra-virgin olive oil
Kosher salt and freshly cracked black pepper
½ cup (1 stick) unsalted butter
½ teaspoon fine sea salt
2½ tablespoons all-purpose flour
4 eggs
Pinch ground nutmeg
Canola oil, for deep frying

VODKA CRÈME FRAÎCHE
1 cup crème fraîche
2 teaspoons vodka
Kosher salt

2 cups lightly packed wild watercress
Flaky sea salt

Prepare the beet "soil." Preheat the oven to 300°F. Wash and gently scrub the beets. Pat dry. Finely slice the beets on a mandoline. Place on a sheet tray and bake for 3 to 4 hours, or until dry. Alternatively, if you have a dehydrator, you can use that to create the beet chips.

Place the dehydrated beets in a food processor, add the pistachios, and process until fine and crumbly. Transfer to a bowl and season with salt and pepper. Add just enough olive oil to moisten the mixture until the texture resembles wet soil. Cover and set aside.

Make the dumplings. Preheat the oven to 375°F. Scrub the potatoes and use a fork to poke holes all over them—this will allow steam to escape. Drizzle with a little olive oil and season with salt. Place on a baking sheet and bake for 45 minutes, or until they are soft. Cut in half down the middle and scoop the flesh out. Pass the flesh through a ricer; there should be about 2 cups of potato puree. Set it aside to cool.

Reduce the oven temperature to 300°F. Line a medium baking dish with parchment paper. Spread the potato puree in the dish and bake for 10 minutes, stirring halfway through, to remove some of the extra moisture.

Combine the butter, sea salt, and ½ cup of water in a medium saucepan. Place over medium-high heat and bring to a boil. When the butter is completely melted, remove from the heat, add the flour all at once, and stir vigorously with a wooden spoon until incorporated. Return to low heat and stir for 1 minute, until the mixture forms a ball and pulls away from the sides of the pan. Still over low heat, stir for 3 more minutes to evaporate more of the moisture.

Transfer the flour mixture to a medium mixing bowl and let cool for 2 minutes. Then add 1 egg and stir with a rubber spatula until well blended. Lightly beat in the second egg, then add the remaining 2 eggs tablespoon by tablespoon, just enough to make the batter smooth. Add the potatoes to the mixture, and season with nutmeg and salt and pepper.

Heat 3 to 4 inches of canola oil in a heavy-bottomed pot to 340°F. Using 2 tablespoons for each dumpling, shape the batter into balls. Working in batches, drop 3 or 4 dumplings at a time into the oil and fry, flipping them occasionally, until puffy, golden, and crisp, about 3 minutes. Remove from the oil with a slotted spoon and drain on a paper towel–lined plate. Season with salt.

Make the vodka crème fraîche. Add the crème fraîche to a mixing bowl and whip with a whisk. Slowly add the vodka, a little at a time, and continue to whip until the mixture is light and creamy. Season lightly with salt.

Arrange the potato dumplings on the beet "soil" and garnish with the watercress and flakes of salt. Serve with the whipped crème fraîche.

vegetable "soil"

Crunchy texture that's interesting on the palate is always a nice element of surprise in a dish. "Soils" can be made out of any vegetable matter that can be dehydrated, but roots seem to work best and also add to the effect of earthiness. But "soils" are more than just a cool garnish. I was having a moment with my sous-chefs a few years ago, frustrated with our rising food costs, and I decided to do something that they would never forget. To make a point I took two garbage bags and spread them out on the floor of the kitchen. I then took two garbage cans filled with perfectly good scrap food from the morning prep shift and dumped them out on the floor. "There are dollar bills in these garbage cans," I said as I picked through two-inch-long carrot nubs, onions, half bunches of herbs, tomatoes, lemons, and peelings from beets. I wrote everything down and gave my sous-chefs a challenge to create "components" or "garnishes" out of what we would normally throw out. The next day we saved anything that was usable and started experimenting. Carrot chips, tomato powder, and this idea, beet "soil," which I really love. Dehydrated beets, pistachios, salt, and a touch of olive oil ground together in a blender looks and tastes faintly of its namesake and has an amazing earthy crunch. Now we go through more of it than our scrap buckets can keep up with.

SWEET POTATO GNOCCHI WITH PORK BOLOGNESE

SERVES 4

PORK BOLOGNESE

1 onion, roughly chopped
¼ fennel bulb, roughly chopped
2 celery ribs, roughly chopped
3 garlic cloves
Extra-virgin olive oil
1½ pounds ground pork
2 sprigs fresh thyme, leaves only
1 sprig fresh rosemary, leaves chopped
2 sprigs fresh oregano, leaves only
2 fresh sage leaves, chopped
2 bay leaves
Kosher salt and freshly cracked black pepper
1 cup dry white wine
3 tablespoons all-purpose flour
3 cups whole milk
3 cups low-sodium chicken stock

SWEET POTATO GNOCCHI

2 pounds sweet potatoes
2 egg yolks
¼ teaspoon freshly grated nutmeg
Kosher salt and freshly cracked black pepper
¾ pound good-quality fresh ricotta, drained
About 1 cup all-purpose flour, plus extra
    for dusting
2 tablespoons unsalted butter

1 handful raw flowering kale
Finely chopped fresh chives
Fresh fennel fronds

Make the Bolognese. Combine the onion, fennel, celery, and garlic in a food processor and pulse until well chopped. Set a large, heavy-bottomed pan over medium heat and add a drizzle of olive oil. Sauté the vegetables for 7 to 8 minutes to cook out some of the moisture. Increase the heat and add the pork. Stir while browning the pork, breaking it up as it cooks. Once browned, add the thyme, rosemary, oregano, sage, and bay leaves and season with salt and pepper. Add the white wine to the pan and cook, stirring, until the wine has reduced, then add the flour and toss to coat the vegetables. Add the milk and chicken stock, and stir to combine. Then reduce the heat and simmer for 1 hour, partially covered. When done, the sauce will be slightly thickened and the meat and vegetables will be very tender.

Make the gnocchi. Preheat the oven to 325°F. Prick the sweet potatoes all over with a fork and arrange on a baking sheet. Roast for 45 to 60 minutes, until the flesh is tender enough to be scooped out with a spoon. Scoop out the warm flesh and pass it through a ricer onto a clean baking sheet. Return to the oven for 10 to 15 minutes to dry out. Let the puree cool slightly, then transfer it to a food processor and puree with the egg yolks, nutmeg, and salt and pepper. In a large mixing bowl, gently fold the sweet potato puree into the ricotta. Then mix in the flour, adding a little at a time until the mixture just forms a light dough that holds together. Do not overwork the dough or add too much flour, or the gnocchi will be tough. Lightly flour a clean work surface. Divide the dough into 3 even portions, and working with one at a time, roll each piece into a rope that is 1 inch in diameter. Cut the ropes into 1-inch pieces and use the back of a fork to roll each piece onto itself and create grooves.

Bring a large pot of salted water to a boil. Cook the gnocchi until they float, 2 to 2½ minutes. Drain and transfer to a plate.

When ready to serve, heat a large nonstick sauté pan over medium-high heat. Add the butter and when it just starts to turn brown and become fragrant, add the gnocchi. Sauté gently, tossing them in the brown butter to coat evenly. Cook until the gnocchi are lightly browned all over.

Serve the gnocchi with the Bolognese sauce and garnish with the kale leaves, chives, and fennel fronds. Drizzle with the brown butter.

WILD ALASKAN SALMON, CARAWAY OIL, FIGS, CRÈME FRAÎCHE, AND TOAST

SERVES 4 TO 6

1 center-cut side of fresh Alaskan salmon
   (about 1½ pounds)

CARAWAY OIL
½ cup grapeseed oil
1 tablespoon caraway seeds
Kosher salt

Extra-virgin olive oil
1 medium yellow onion, thinly sliced
Flaky sea salt
6 ripe California Mission figs
1 cup crème fraîche
1 ficelle (thin baguette)
1 tablespoon fresh thyme leaves
½ bunch hydroponic watercress

Prepare the salmon. Clean the salmon and use tweezers to remove any pin bones. Using a sharp knife, cut the salmon into ½-inch-thick pieces on a severe bias to yield wide strips. Working with one piece at a time, place the salmon between two sheets of plastic wrap and gently pound, using the flat side of a meat tenderizer, working carefully from the center outward so the fillet remains intact. Work the salmon into the shape of your plate so it fits neatly within the perimeter. Transfer the pounded fillets to individual plates and chill.

Prepare the caraway oil. In a medium sauté pan, combine the grapeseed oil and caraway seeds. Warm gently over medium heat until fragrant and the seeds are lightly toasted, 3 to 4 minutes. Season with salt. Transfer to a small bowl and set aside to cool.

Return the pan to medium-high heat and coat it with olive oil. Add the onion and sauté for 5 to 7 minutes, until well caramelized. Season with sea salt, and set aside to cool. Cut the figs into quarters through the stem. Whip the crème fraîche with a whisk until light and aerated.

Make the toasts. Preheat the oven to 350°F. Slice the ficelle into ¼-inch-thick slices and set them out on a baking sheet. Drizzle with olive oil and toast for 6 to 7 minutes, until golden and crispy.

To assemble, use a pastry brush to smear the salmon with the caraway oil and seeds. Top with some onion, a scoop of whipped crème fraîche, toast slices, and figs. Garnish with the thyme leaves and watercress.

wild salmon

The steep decline in the number of wild California salmon may seem to be a recent and unexplainable phenomenon, but they have been steadily disappearing from North American waters for more than 160 years. In the early 1800s the northwestern United States and southern British Columbia were literally awash with chinook, coho, chum, pink sockeye, masu, steelhead, and coastal cutthroat trout. Beautiful and poetic in natural design, they migrated thousands of miles from the open ocean of the northern Pacific Rim to the intercoastal estuaries and rivers deep into North America to spawn.

As Europeans settled North America, control over the waterways became crucial, as natural resources like beaver pelts and whale blubber were shipped out of the New World. Pools created by beaver dams were natural oases for spawning salmon; with beavers being trapped at record numbers and their dams smashed to provide boat passage, the salmon began to struggle. At the same time whaling towns were popping up virtually overnight at the mouths of rivers in the Pacific Northwest, introducing the salmon runs to a new predator: humans.

The great gold rush, followed by the invention of hydroelectric turbines used to convert water current into electricity, produced a period of major industrial growth as well as a naive and wasteful sense of entitlement toward what seemed like unlimited natural resources that decimated the salmon population.

The big picture is the loss of carcass biomass. Since a salmon's final act is spawning new life, the carcasses they leave behind provide irreplaceable nutrients for an entire ecosystem. Seals, eagles, wolves, bears, raccoons, crab, and ancient Native Americans have all depended on salmon for nutrients, and they provided essential nitrogen for tiny phytoplankton and the giant redwoods of California. Wild salmon are a life-giving, precious natural resource; it's only logical that their loss can bring about the collapse of the entire ecosystem. Saving wild salmon from extinction is, in effect, saving ourselves. Get involved. Check out wildsalmoncenter.org for more information.

SALMON TARTARE USUYAKI, FRESH CUCUMBER, AND MISO MAYO

EGG CRÈPES
3 large eggs
3 tablespoons dashi (Japanese broth)
2 tablespoons vodka
½ teaspoon sugar
¼ teaspoon kosher salt
Nonstick cooking spray

SALMON TARTARE
1 pound boneless, skinless salmon fillet
½ teaspoon fresh lemon juice
¼ teaspoon toasted sesame oil
Kosher salt
½ cup mayonnaise

MISO MAYO
1 cup mayonnaise
1 tablespoon white miso
2 tablespoons bonito flakes
1 teaspoon fresh lemon juice
1 teaspoon toasted sesame oil

CHILE OIL
1 tablespoon sambal oelek
½ cup grapeseed oil
Pinch grated lemon zest
½ lemon
Kosher salt

1 hothouse cucumber, cut into wedges
2 Persian cucumbers, cut into wedges
Pulp of 1 lemon cucumber, scooped out
    with a spoon

Fresh mint leaves
Fresh chives, cut into 2-inch pieces,
    and chive flowers
Fresh chervil leaves
Flaky sea salt
Pimentón

Make the crèpes. Combine the eggs, dashi, vodka, sugar, and salt in a bowl and whisk together. Set aside for 10 minutes or so to settle and allow the bubbles to subside. Set a 9-inch nonstick skillet over low-medium heat and spray it with nonstick cooking spray. Add enough egg mixture to just cover the bottom of the pan completely in a thin layer. Cook for 10 to 15 seconds, then remove from the heat — the crèpe needs to cook on only one side and you don't want it to take on any color. Transfer it to a plate and continue making crèpes; you should have 4 or 5 crèpes. Trim each crèpe into a neat square shape.

Make the salmon tartare. Using a sharp knife, cut the salmon into very small cubes and place in a mixing bowl. Toss with the lemon juice, sesame oil, and salt. Then lightly dress with just enough mayonnaise to coat the salmon and help it hold together.

Form the rolls. Lay each crèpe on a piece of plastic wrap. Make a line of salmon tartare along one edge, then fold the ends in and roll the crèpe tightly, burrito-style. Wrap tightly in plastic wrap and refrigerate for 10 to 15 minutes so they chill and will be easier to cut.

Make the miso mayonnaise. In a blender, combine the mayonnaise, miso, bonito flakes, lemon juice, and sesame oil. Blend until the bonito flakes are completely incorporated.

Make the chile oil. Mix the sambal oelek with the grapeseed oil, lemon zest, and a squeeze of lemon juice. Season with salt and set aside.

Cut the salmon rolls into 1½-inch pieces and serve with the cucumber wedges, lemon cucumber pulp, miso mayo, and chile oil. Garnish with mint leaves, chives, and chervil leaves. Season with flaky sea salt and pimentón.

SEARED SCALLOPS, TOMATO-CHILE JAM, FRESH PEAS, AND BACON

SERVES 4

TOMATO-CHILE JAM

1 tablespoon tomato paste
1 (14-ounce) can crushed San Marzano tomatoes
½ cup chopped roasted Jimmy Nardello
    peppers, crushed to a pulp with a mortar
    and pestle and a little olive oil
⅓ cup sugar
Kosher salt and freshly cracked black pepper
2 tablespoons red wine vinegar

1 cup fresh English peas
Kosher salt
Grapeseed oil
8 thin slices applewood-smoked bacon
16 diver scallops
Fleur de sel
Fresh basil leaves
Fresh pea tendrils

Make the tomato-chile jam. In a medium saucepan, stir together the tomato paste, tomatoes and their juices, peppers, sugar, and ¼ cup of water. Set over medium heat and simmer for 20 to 25 minutes to allow the flavors to come together. Once reduced and thick, season with salt and pepper and add the red wine vinegar. Puree with a stick blender until it has a consistent, slightly chunky texture. Allow to cool slightly.

Add the peas and ¼ cup of water to a small saucepan and set over high heat. Season lightly with salt and steam the peas for 1 minute, until they turn bright green. Drain and set aside.

Make the lardons. Set a large sauté pan over high heat and coat it with grapeseed oil. Slice the bacon on the bias to yield long, thin strips. Add to the hot pan and cook for 5 to 6 minutes, stirring as they cook so they curl into twisted, crisped lardons. Then transfer to a paper towel–lined plate. Pour the rendered bacon fat into a small bowl and reserve.

Cook the scallops. Wipe out the sauté pan and set it back over medium-high heat. Pat the scallops dry with paper towels and season with kosher salt. Coat the hot pan with grapeseed oil. Cook the scallops undisturbed for 2 to 3 minutes, until golden brown. Remove from the heat and turn the scallops to barely cook on the second side, 30 seconds. Remove from the pan.

Serve the scallops with a smear of the tomato-chile jam. Season with fleur de sel. Top with the bacon lardons, steamed peas, basil, and pea tendrils. Drizzle the reserved bacon fat around the plate.

SEARED SCALLOPS, LEMON GNOCCHI, AND FAVAS

SERVES 4

LEMON GNOCCHI
6½ pounds Russet potatoes
Extra-virgin olive oil
Sea salt
1½ to 2 cups all-purpose flour, plus extra
    for dusting
Grated zest of 2 lemons
1 egg yolk

1 pound fresh fava beans (whole pods)
4 tablespoons (½ stick) unsalted butter,
    cut into cubes
¼ cup extra-virgin olive oil
Flaky sea salt

SCALLOPS
Grapeseed oil
24 bay scallops
Kosher salt and freshly cracked black pepper

Finely chopped fresh chives
Micro arugula

Make the gnocchi. Preheat the oven to 350°F. Scrub the potatoes and pat dry. Pierce the skins all over with a fork, drizzle with olive oil and sea salt, and place on a baking sheet. Roast for 45 minutes to 1 hour, until they are easily pierced with a paring knife. (Do not turn off the oven.) Allow the potatoes to cool slightly, then peel them while they are still hot. Press the potatoes through a ricer. Spread the riced potato on a sheet pan and place in the oven for 10 to 15 minutes to dry out.

Transfer the potatoes to a large bowl and add 1½ cups of the flour, the lemon zest, and egg yolk. Mix with your hands, adding more flour as needed, until the mixture just holds together as a mass. Do not overwork the dough.

Transfer the potato dough to a lightly floured surface. Divide the dough into 2 or 3 pieces and gently roll each portion into a ¾-inch-diameter rope. Add flour as necessary to keep the dough from sticking and to help form the rope shape. Cut the rope into 1-inch-long pieces. Gently roll each piece into a ball, then shape it into an oval using the back of a fork. The finished gnocchi should be marked with ridges (this will help the pillows hold the sauce). Chill the gnocchi in the refrigerator for 10 to 15 minutes (uncovered) to firm up.

Poach the fava beans. Bring a large pot of salted water to a boil. Add the fava beans and boil for 2 to 3 minutes, until just cooked and tender. Drain, then plunge the favas into a large bowl of salted ice water. Remove the cooled favas from the pods, and then remove the thin green membrane from each bean. Set aside until ready to serve.

Poach the gnocchi. Put the butter, olive oil, and sea salt in a large bowl. Bring a large pot of salted water to a boil. Poach the gnocchi for 2 to 3 minutes, until they float to the surface. Remove and drain with a slotted spoon, and add directly to the bowl containing the butter and olive oil. Add a splash of the cooking water and swirl the gnocchi around so the butter melts and the water, butter, and olive oil form a sauce that coats each gnocchi. Fold in the poached fava beans.

Cook the scallops. Set a large sauté pan over high heat and add a drizzle of grapeseed oil. Pat the scallops dry and season with salt and pepper. Add the scallops and cook for 1 minute without moving, until they are nice and golden. Flip the scallops to finish cooking on the second side, about 30 seconds.

Serve the seared scallops with the gnocchi and fava beans. Drizzle with the gnocchi pan sauce and garnish with chives and micro arugula.

SALT-SEARED SHRIMP, BLACK-EYED PEAS, OKRA PICKLES, AND CHILE AIOLI

SERVES 2 TO 4

PICKLED OKRA
1 cup white vinegar
¼ cup sugar
1 bay leaf
1 teaspoon dried red pepper flakes
1 teaspoon yellow mustard seeds
Kosher salt and freshly ground black pepper
1 pound fresh okra

CHILE AIOLI
2 egg whites
1 roasted Jimmy Nardello pepper
¼ teaspoon Dijon mustard
2 tablespoons fresh lemon juice
½ teaspoon grated lemon zest
¼ teaspoon kosher salt
¼ teaspoon sugar
1 cup grapeseed oil

BLACK-EYED PEAS
1½ cups dried black-eyed peas
2 lemon slices
Kosher salt
¼ cup extra-virgin olive oil
2 tablespoons fresh lemon juice

CURRY OIL
2 tablespoons curry powder
⅓ cup grapeseed oil
Kosher salt

SHRIMP
12 jumbo shrimp in the shell
Fleur de sel

¼ cup flowering basil
Fleur de sel

Pickle the okra. In a small saucepan, combine the vinegar, sugar, bay leaf, red pepper flakes, mustard seeds, salt, pepper, and 1 cup of water. Bring to a boil and stir until the sugar has dissolved completely and the brine is fragrant. Allow to cool. Place the okra in a vacuum-seal bag, pour the cooled brine over it, and seal on the highest pressure setting.

Make the chile aioli. In a blender, combine the egg whites, pepper, mustard, lemon juice, lemon zest, salt, and sugar. With the blender running, add the grapeseed oil in a slow, steady stream so the mixture emulsifies. Refrigerate until ready to serve.

Cook the black-eyed peas. Rinse the black-eyed peas under cold running water. Drain, and place in a large pot with the lemon slices and salt. Add water to cover by 2 to 3 inches. Cook for 1 hour, or until the peas are tender, then drain and discard the lemon slices. Place the peas in a large mixing bowl and dress with the extra-virgin olive oil and lemon juice.

Make the curry oil. Combine the curry powder and grapeseed oil in a small saucepan. Season with salt and warm the oil over medium heat to toast the spices. When fragrant, remove from the heat and allow to cool.

Cook the shrimp. Prepare the shrimp by splitting them down the back with a sharp knife. Remove and discard the vein. Season the shrimp all over with a liberal amount of fleur de sel. Set a dry cast-iron pan over high heat and when it is smoking hot, add the shrimp. Cook on the first side for 2 to 3 minutes. Turn the shrimp and cook for 1 more minute, until they are cooked through and well charred on the outside.

Drain the okra and slice the pods in half lengthwise. Serve the shrimp with the black-eyed peas, okra, and chile aioli. Drizzle with the curry oil and garnish with flowering basil and fleur de sel.

BALSAMIC-GLAZED CALIFORNIA SQUAB, CRUSHED CLEMENTINE, AND GRITS

SERVES 4

GRITS
1½ cups heavy cream
1 cup stone-ground grits
Kosher salt and freshly cracked black pepper
2 tablespoons unsalted butter
½ cup grated Parmigiano-Reggiano

CRUSHED CLEMENTINES
6 clementines
1 tablespoon sugar
⅓ cup extra-virgin olive oil
Kosher salt and freshly cracked black pepper

SQUAB
4 whole semi-boneless squabs
    (10 to 12 ounces each)
4 tablespoons extra-virgin olive oil
½ cup walnut halves
16 fresh sage leaves
Kosher salt and freshly cracked black pepper
1 cup balsamic vinegar
2 teaspoons honey
2 teaspoons fresh lemon juice
2 tablespoons cold unsalted butter,
    cut into cubes

¾ cup pitted green olives, hand-crushed

Make the grits. Set a large saucepan over high heat and add the cream and 2½ cups of water. Bring to a boil, then add the grits and whisk well. Season with salt and pepper, then reduce the heat and simmer for 30 to 35 minutes, stirring every 2 to 3 minutes. When the grits are smooth, creamy, and fragrant, remove from the heat and add the butter and Parmesan. Stir to incorporate and melt. Keep warm.

Prepare the clementines. Roughly chop the clementines (skin and all). Use a mortar and pestle to gently crush them together with the sugar, olive oil, and salt and pepper until they are a pulpy mass. Set aside.

Prepare the squab. Preheat the oven to 375°F. Using a sharp knife, remove the legs from each bird. Separate the drumsticks from the thighs. Then cut each breast away from the carcass. You should have 6 pieces (2 thighs, 2 legs, 2 boneless breast portions) from each bird.

Set a large ovenproof sauté pan over high heat and add 2 tablespoons of the olive oil. Add the walnuts and sage leaves and fry, tossing often, for 3 to 4 minutes, until crispy and brown. Drain on paper towels. Coat the pan with the remaining 2 tablespoons oil and season the squab portions all over with salt and pepper. Place the pieces skin-side down in the pan and sear until well browned, 3 to 4 minutes. Turn the pieces over, transfer the pan to the oven, and bake for 20 minutes.

Make the balsamic glaze. Transfer the roasted squab to a platter to rest, and reheat the sauté pan on medium heat for about 2 minutes. Deglaze with the balsamic and 2 tablespoons of water. Simmer to reduce the sauce by half, then remove from the heat, season with salt and pepper, and add the honey, lemon juice, and cold butter cubes. Swirl to incorporate the butter and give the sauce a nice richness and sheen. Return the squab pieces to the pan over low heat and baste with the sauce.

Serve the squab with the grits, and garnish with the crushed clementines, green olives, toasted walnuts, and crispy sage. Drizzle with the balsamic reduction.

PEACH AND PROSCIUTTO SALAD WITH HOMEMADE BURRATA

SERVES 4 TO 6

HOMEMADE BURRATA
2 pounds fresh mozzarella curd, at room
    temperature
¼ teaspoon kosher salt
1 pint heavy cream

8 thin slices prosciutto (about ½ pound)
2 firm but ripe yellow peaches,
    pitted and quartered
2 firm but ripe white peaches,
    pitted and quartered
Micro arugula
¼ cup extra-virgin olive oil
2 teaspoons fresh lemon juice
Flaky sea salt
Freshly cracked black pepper

Make the burrata. Cut the mozzarella curd into cubes and place them in a large bowl. Add the salt, then pour the cream over the top. Use a wooden spoon to lightly fold the cream and curd together. Pour enough hot water (about 170°F) over the top to just lightly melt the curds. Then stir 4 to 5 times to stretch the curd until it begins to come together as a single, shiny mass. Using your hands, remove the mass from the liquid and place it in a bowl.

Prepare the prosciutto. Preheat the oven to 350°F. Lay the prosciutto slices flat in a single layer on a baking sheet. Bake for 15 to 20 minutes, until crispy and golden. Drain on paper towels.

To assemble, use a big spoon to scoop up portions of fresh burrata. Serve with the peach wedges and top with the crispy prosciutto and micro arugula. Dress with the olive oil, the lemon juice, sea salt, and a few turns of cracked black pepper.

SUMMER PLUMS WITH FOIE GRAS, CORN FRITTERS, AND MÂCHE

SERVES 4

1 tablespoon sugar
2 lemon slices
4 firm but ripe mixed yellow and purple plums

FOIE GRAS MOUSSE

1 pound foie gras, trimmed of any veins or
    blemishes
Flaky sea salt and freshly cracked black pepper
Juice of 1 lemon
¼ cup heavy cream

CORN FRITTERS

4 ears fresh corn
1 medium shallot, minced
2 eggs
1 cup rice flour
1½ teaspoons baking powder
1 teaspoon finely chopped fresh marjoram
Kosher salt and freshly cracked black pepper
Grapeseed oil, for deep frying

4 cups lightly packed mâche
1 tablespoon fresh marjoram leaves
Kosher salt
Flaky sea salt
Freshly cracked black pepper

Prepare the plums. Combine ½ cup of water with the sugar and lemon slices in a small saucepan. Bring to a simmer over high heat and stir until the sugar is dissolved, about 1 minute. Remove from the heat and allow to cool. Split the plums in half, discard the stones, and cut each plum into quarters. Place the plums in a single layer in a vacuum-seal bag and add the lemon syrup. Seal on the highest pressure setting.

Prepare the foie gras. Slice the foie gras into 1-inch-thick slices and return to the refrigerator for 10 minutes to firm up again. Place a large skillet over very high heat. Season the foie gras liberally with salt, and sear in the hot pan until it is just golden, about 1 minute per side. Remove from the pan and set aside to cool in the fridge, 10 to 12 minutes. Add half of the lemon juice to the pan with the residual foie gras fat, and swirl to make a light dressing. Reserve and set aside.

In a food processor, combine the seared foie gras, remaining lemon juice, and salt and pepper. Puree until smooth, then add the cream and puree again. Transfer the mousse to a small dish and cover tightly with plastic wrap to prevent oxidation. Refrigerate until set, about 1 hour.

Make the corn fritters. Husk the corn and use a sharp knife to slice off the kernels. Combine two-thirds of the corn kernels with the shallot, eggs, flour, baking powder, marjoram, and salt and pepper in a food processor. Blend until well combined, about 20 seconds, scraping down the bowl as required. Transfer to a mixing bowl, fold in the reserved corn kernels, and mix well. Heat 4 to 5 inches of grapeseed oil to 350°F in a large pot. Working in batches, use a large spoon to drop dollops of the batter into the hot oil and fry for 3 to 4 minutes, until golden brown. Use a strainer to remove from the oil, and drain on a paper towel–lined plate. Season with salt.

Serve the fritters with spoonfuls of foie gras mousse, the pressed plums, and a garnish of mâche and marjoram. Season the reserved dressing with kosher salt, and drizzle over each plate. Finish with flakes of sea salt and cracked black pepper.

california stone fruits

With all due respect to Georgia farmers, their peaches can't hold a candle to California stone fruits. The flavor of fully ripened California peaches, plums, and especially apricots is transcendent, unlike that of any common commodity fruit I've tasted in the United States. The flavor comes from the arid climate and low rainfall in California's farm regions, where the sustainable practice of dry farming (that is, without irrigation) is common. Dry farming is not a strategy for maximizing yield, but it produces fruit of impeccable quality. It's been practiced for thousands of years in the Mediterranean with olives and grapes, and Spanish explorers planted apricots in California as far back as the mid-eighteenth century.

California soil, soaked to the bone for most of the winter and spring (up to twenty inches in some years), is rocky, deep, and well drained, with a perfect pH balance. The Mediterranean climate, cool nights, and warm California sun do the rest. When the rainy season ends, usually in late April, the California landscape is lush and green. The water sits deep in the soil, resulting in orchards that are by nature hardy, struggling to pull moisture from the ground and convert energy from the leaves through photosynthesis. The trees have no choice but to be prudent with their energy, perpetuating their species with less but better fruit, naturally selected.

East Coast peach trees, due to consistent rainfall throughout the growing season, produce heavier fruit that can end up plumped with water and, in my opinion, lacking in flavor. California fruit is dense, with a soft, candylike fiber and a juicy flavor that is almost surreal. At my restaurants we take that density to the next level by compressing the fruit with a few tablespoons of lemon simple syrup. The acid from the simple syrup is pulled into the center of each apricot wedge through vacuum compression, leaving a perfectly balanced bite of apricot jam that is translucent, with a glorious yellow-orange color as vibrant as the California sun. You can compress stone fruits in your own kitchen the same way, with a simple vacuum sealer.

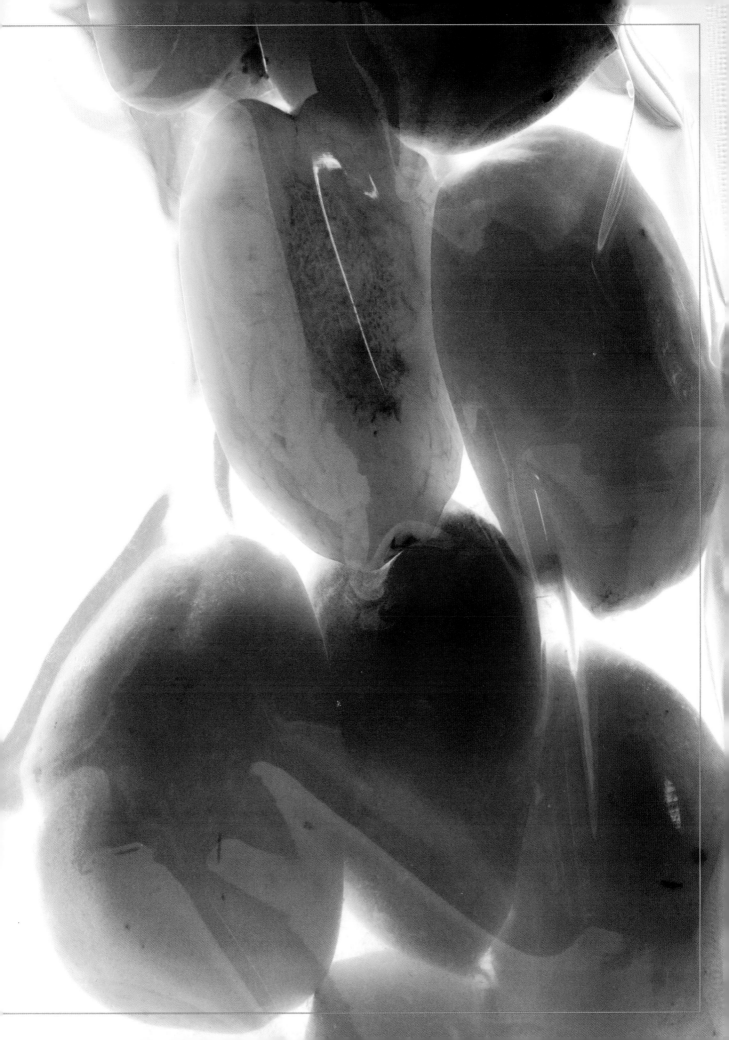

TOMATOES, MAYONNAISE, BASIL, AND TOAST

SERVES 4

FRESH MAYO

2 egg whites
¼ teaspoon Dijon mustard
2 teaspoons fresh lemon juice
¼ teaspoon kosher salt
¼ teaspoon sugar
1 cup grapeseed oil

1 pound assorted heirloom, Roma,
   and cherry tomatoes
Extra-virgin olive oil
Flaky sea salt
Freshly cracked black pepper
4 thick slices sourdough bread
Small fresh basil leaves

Make the mayo. In a blender, combine the egg whites, mustard, lemon juice, salt, and sugar. Blend until smooth. With the blender running, add the grapeseed oil in a slow, steady stream so the mixture emulsifies. Refrigerate until ready to serve.

Prepare the tomatoes. Cut the larger tomatoes into small wedges and bite-size pieces. Slice the Roma tomatoes. Heat 2 inches of olive oil to 375°F in a large pot. Place the cherry tomatoes in a wire mesh skimmer and submerge it in the hot oil for 2 to 3 seconds, just until the skins burst. Remove from the oil and season with flaky sea salt. Toss the cherry tomatoes with the other tomatoes. Dress with a little olive oil and season with a turn of cracked black pepper.

Preheat a gas or charcoal grill or grill pan. Drizzle olive oil over the bread slices and grill for 1 minute per side, until crispy and charred around the edges but still soft in the middle. Serve the tomatoes on the grilled bread with olive oil and dots of the mayonnaise; garnish with the reserved tomato caviar and fresh basil.

NOTE Roma tomatoes are fun. If you like, before slicing them cut off ¼ inch from the stem end and use a small spoon to remove the seed clusters (known as "tomato caviar"); use these for garnish.

frying tomatoes

An easy way to peel tomatoes that actually improves their flavor is a quick blanching in hot oil. When dropped into 375°F oil, the flesh of the tomato produces a quick shot of steam that pushes the skin off in a matter of seconds. Since it happens so fast (and because oil and water don't mix), you lose zero flavor in the process. By comparison, when you blanch a tomato in boiling water at the relatively lower temperature of 212°F, yes, you peel the tomato, but you also release an enormous amount of tomato flavor into the water. Frying in oil also creates a cool little garnish we call firecracker tomatoes because they look like they exploded—and who doesn't love fireworks?

CHERRY TOMATO AND COCONUT SALAD

SERVES 4

MINT VINEGAR

1 cup white vinegar
⅓ cup sugar
½ teaspoon kosher salt
1 cup lightly packed fresh mint leaves

2 pints assorted small tomatoes
4 Persian cucumbers

FRIED SHALLOTS

2 cups olive oil
1 shallot, thinly sliced
½ cup all-purpose flour
Kosher salt

VINAIGRETTE

½ cup prepared mint vinegar
1 tablespoon fish sauce
1 Thai bird chile, finely sliced
2 teaspoons toasted sesame oil
1 teaspoon honey
1 small garlic clove, smashed
2 fresh ginger slices, smashed

½ cup shaved fresh young coconut
Fresh cilantro leaves
2 tablespoons thinly sliced fresh mint leaves
¼ cup roasted peanuts, split

Make the mint vinegar. In a medium saucepan, combine the vinegar, sugar, and salt with ¼ cup of water. Bring to a simmer and stir until the sugar has completely dissolved. Remove from the heat and add the mint leaves (squeeze them in your hand to bruise the leaves before adding them; this will allow more of its flavor to infuse the solution). Set aside and allow to cool.

Prepare the tomatoes and cucumbers. Bring a large pot of water to a boil. Place a large bowl of ice water near the pot. Using the tip of a paring knife, make a small "x" incision in the bottom of each tomato. Add the tomatoes to the boiling water and blanch for 8 to 10 seconds, until the skin starts to wilt. Remove with a strainer and immediately plunge into the ice water. Remove, and discard the skins. Place the tomatoes in a vacuum-seal bag and cover with some of the cooled mint vinegar. Seal on medium pressure to quickly pickle. Thinly slice the Persian cucumbers and add to a second vacuum-seal bag. Cover with cooled mint vinegar, and seal on medium pressure to quickly pickle. When ready to use, remove the tomatoes and cucumbers from the bags and drain off the brine.

Fry the shallots. Heat the olive oil in a small skillet to 350°F. Lightly dredge the shallot rounds in flour, and fry in the hot oil for 2 to 3 minutes, until golden brown. Drain on paper towels and season immediately with salt.

Make the vinaigrette. Combine all the vinaigrette ingredients in a bowl and whisk together.

Place the shaved coconut on a plate. Set the pickled tomatoes and cucumbers on top of and around the coconut. Garnish with cilantro, mint, peanuts, and the fried shallots. Drizzle with the vinaigrette.

CALIFORNIA TUNA CRUDO WITH CRUSHED PINEAPPLE, CHILE, AND SOY

SERVES 4

2½ cups diced fresh pineapple
2 teaspoons fresh lemon juice

SOY DRESSING
1 tablespoon white miso
1 teaspoon low-sodium soy sauce
2 tablespoons fresh lemon juice
1 teaspoon sugar
¼ cup grapeseed oil

CHILE OIL
5 tablespoons grapeseed oil
1 tablespoon toasted sesame oil
2 teaspoons dried red pepper flakes

½ pound fresh albacore tuna, thinly sliced
    across the grain
1 tablespoon toasted white sesame seeds
2 scallions, green part only, finely sliced
8 to 10 cilantro sprigs

Prepare the pineapple. Place half the pineapple cubes in a blender. Add the lemon juice and ¼ cup of water and puree until completely smooth. Set aside. Use a mortar and pestle to crush the remaining pineapple chunks until they are broken down but still have a bit of texture.

Make the soy dressing. Combine the miso, soy, lemon juice, sugar, grapeseed oil, and 2 tablespoons of water in a blender. Puree until smooth and slightly emulsified.

Make the chile oil. Combine the grapeseed and sesame oils and red pepper flakes in a small saucepan. Warm over medium heat for 8 to 10 minutes without allowing the oil to simmer. Then remove from the heat and cool to room temperature.

Divide the tuna among 4 chilled plates, arranging the slices so they overlap slightly. Top with the crushed pineapple and sprinkle with the toasted sesame seeds. Drizzle with the pineapple puree, soy dressing, and chile oil. Garnish with the sliced scallion tops and the cilantro.

SUMMER SQUASH CRUDO, RAW TUNA, CHARRED ONION, WHITE MISO, AND SUNFLOWER

SERVES 4

MISO DRESSING
3 tablespoons white miso
2 tablespoons seasoned rice vinegar
1 tablespoon honey
3 tablespoons grapeseed oil
Kosher salt

1 small white onion

1 (1-pound) piece of center-cut sushi-grade
    tuna loin
2 or 3 assorted medium squash (zucchini,
    summer squash, lemon squash)
2 to 3 tablespoons toasted sunflower seeds
¼ cup sunflower sprouts
2 teaspoons toasted black mustard seeds
Flaky sea salt

Make the miso dressing. Combine all the dressing ingredients in a large bowl and mix well with a whisk.

Prepare the onion. Preheat the broiler. Peel the onion, slice it into ¼-inch-thick rings, and place in a large bowl. Toss the onion slices with a few tablespoons of the miso dressing to coat evenly and separate the rings. Transfer to a roasting pan and broil for 5 to 6 minutes, until caramelized and slightly charred; stir halfway through so they cook evenly. Set aside.

Prepare the tuna and squash. Cut the tuna loin into 1-inch cubes. Set aside 2 tablespoons of the miso dressing, and toss the tuna in the remaining dressing. Slice the squash into thin disks on a mandoline or with a sharp knife.

To assemble, arrange the squash slices in a single layer on a plate. Top with the charred onions and the tuna cubes. Garnish with the sunflower seeds, sunflower sprouts, and toasted mustard seeds. Drizzle with the reserved miso dressing and finish with flaky sea salt.

ZUCCHINI, PICKLED CHERRIES, RICOTTA, AND BASIL WITH PAN-ROASTED PORK CHOP

SERVES 2

1 cup good-quality fresh ricotta

PORK CHOPS
1 cup kosher salt
½ cup sugar
8 sprigs fresh thyme
4 sprigs fresh rosemary
1 bay leaf
½ lemon
2 double-cut pork loin chops (1 bone,
    about 1½ inches thick, 1 pound each)
Kosher salt and freshly cracked black pepper
Grapeseed oil

2 zucchini or summer squash

PICKLED CHERRIES
1 cup champagne vinegar
1 cup sugar
1 cinnamon stick
1 teaspoon yellow mustard seeds
3 or 4 black peppercorns
1 bay leaf
2 cups pitted red cherries

Fresh basil leaves and buds
Freshly cracked black pepper

Drain the ricotta. Line a strainer with 2 layers of cheesecloth and add the ricotta. Drain over a bowl for 30 minutes, twisting the cheesecloth occasionally to press out as much liquid as possible.

Brine the pork chops. In a large container, combine 7 cups of water with the salt, sugar, thyme, rosemary, bay leaf, and lemon. Mix together with a whisk until the sugar dissolves. Add the pork chops and refrigerate for 30 minutes.

Cook the pork chops. Preheat the oven to 375°F. Remove the chops from the brine and pat dry very thoroughly. Season with salt and pepper. Set a large cast-iron pan over high heat and coat it with grapeseed oil. When it is smoking, add the pork chops and cook for 8 to 10 minutes, until well browned. Cut the zucchini into ¼-inch-thick slices. Turn the chops over and add the zucchini to the pan. Transfer the pan to the oven and roast for 8 to 9 minutes, until the internal temperature of the pork reaches 140° to 145°F for medium.

Pickle the cherries. Bring the vinegar, sugar, cinnamon stick, mustard seeds, peppercorns, bay leaf, and 1 cup of water to a simmer in a medium saucepan over high heat. Stir well, and once the sugar has dissolved, remove from the heat and set aside to cool slightly. Place the cherries in a vacuum-seal bag and pour the cooled brine over them. Seal the bag on the highest pressure setting. Remove the cherries from the bag and reserve the pickling liquid.

Make the sauce. Remove the pork and zucchini from the pan and set aside. Add some of the cherry pickling juice to the pan and stir well with the pan drippings to make a broken vinaigrette. Season with salt and pepper.

Serve the pork chops and zucchini drizzled with the vinaigrette. Garnish with the crumbled ricotta, pickled cherries, and basil. Finish with plenty of cracked black pepper.

ZUCCHINI RICOTTA FRITTERS WITH GRAPEFRUIT AIOLI, PINE NUTS, AND BASIL

SERVES 4 TO 6

2 medium zucchini
Extra-virgin olive oil
Kosher salt and freshly cracked black pepper
2 cups good-quality fresh ricotta
1 cup all-purpose flour
2 eggs, beaten
2 cups panko bread crumbs

GRAPEFRUIT AIOLI

2 egg whites
¼ teaspoon kosher salt
¼ teaspoon Dijon mustard
½ teaspoon grated ruby grapefruit zest
1 tablespoon fresh ruby grapefruit juice
½ teaspoon sugar
1 cup grapeseed oil

2 quarts canola oil
Kosher salt
8 fresh zucchini blossoms
¼ cup fresh basil leaves
¼ cup toasted pine nuts
Extra-virgin olive oil
Freshly cracked black pepper

Make the zucchini chips. Preheat the oven to 350°F. Using a mandoline, slice off 2 to 3 long thin strips from either side of each zucchini, for 8 to 12 strips in all. Reserve the inner portions. Lay the zucchini strips on a baking sheet and drizzle with a little olive oil. Bake for 15 to 20 minutes, until golden and slightly curled around the edges. Season with salt.

Make the fritters. Cut the interior zucchini pieces into thin strips. Line a baking sheet with a kitchen towel and arrange the zucchini strips on it in a single layer. Sprinkle with salt, and set aside for 15 minutes to draw the moisture out and make the strips pliable. If the ricotta is very moist, strain it through several layers of cheesecloth, pressing out as much moisture as possible. Transfer the ricotta to a bowl and season with salt and pepper.

Set up a breading station with separate shallow bowls for the flour, eggs, and panko. Season the flour and panko generously with salt and pepper. Place approximately 2 teaspoons of the ricotta at the end of one zucchini strip and roll it up. Roll the fritter first in the seasoned flour, then in the egg, and finally in the seasoned panko. Repeat with all the remaining zucchini strips and refrigerate for 15 minutes to set the coating.

Make the grapefruit aioli. In a blender, combine the egg whites, salt, mustard, grapefruit zest and juice, and sugar, and blend until just foamy. With the blender running, add the grapeseed oil in a slow, steady stream to create a thin, mayonnaise-like sauce. Chill until ready to serve.

Cook the fritters and zucchini blossoms. Fill a deep saucepan two-thirds full with canola oil and heat it to 350°F. Add the fritters, 5 or 6 at a time, and fry until golden and crispy, 6 to 7 minutes. Drain on paper towels and season immediately with salt.

In the same oil, deep-fry the zucchini blossoms for 1 to 2 minutes, until golden and slightly transparent. Drain on paper towels and season immediately with salt.

To serve, place the fritters, blossoms, fresh basil leaves, and pine nuts on a plate. Dot with the grapefruit aioli and extra-virgin olive oil, and finish with some cracked black pepper. Scatter the zucchini chips over the top.

WHOLE WHEAT PASTA, ZUCCHINI PUREE, SUMMER SQUASH, TOMATOES, AND OREGANO

SERVES 4

½ cup raw pine nuts
Kosher salt and freshly cracked black pepper
1 pint grape tomatoes
Extra-virgin olive oil

ZUCCHINI PUREE

6 medium zucchini
3 large pattypan squash
1 large shallot
Extra-virgin olive oil
Kosher salt and freshly cracked black pepper
1 tablespoon fresh lemon juice

1 pound fresh whole wheat spaghetti
Kosher salt and freshly cracked black pepper
½ cup shaved ricotta salata
Fresh oregano buds
Fleur de sel
Extra-virgin olive oil

Toast the pine nuts. Set a large sauté pan over medium heat. Add the pine nuts and toast for about 5 minutes while stirring, until they are fragrant and golden brown all over. Season lightly with salt.

Dry the tomatoes. Preheat the oven to 350°F. Split the grape tomatoes in half lengthwise and set them out on a baking sheet, cut-side up. Drizzle with olive oil and season with salt and pepper. Roast for 25 to 30 minutes, until just wilted. Remove and set aside.

Make the zucchini puree. Cut the zucchini into ½-inch slices and cut the pattypan squash into bite-size pieces. Dice the shallot. Place the vegetables on a baking sheet, drizzle with olive oil, and season with salt and pepper. Roast for 20 to 25 minutes, until the vegetables are tender and lightly caramelized around the edges. Reserve about 2 cups of the roasted vegetables, and transfer the rest to a food processor. Add the lemon juice, about ¼ cup of olive oil, and salt and pepper, and puree until smooth. Thin with a little water if required; the puree should be light and smooth.

Cook the pasta. Bring a large pot of salted water to a rolling boil. Add the pasta and cook for 4 to 5 minutes, until just al dente. Drain the pasta, return it to the pot, and fold in the vegetable puree. Toss to coat everything evenly. Season with salt and pepper.

To serve, take a carving fork and twirl the pasta around the tines. Slide the pasta off onto a plate for a neat presentation. Top with the reserved roasted vegetables, roasted tomatoes, toasted pine nuts, and ricotta salata. Garnish with the oregano and a sprinkle of fleur de sel. Drizzle with olive oil.

dehydrating

Dehydrating is a technique as old as humanity, and it's a very effective way to coax out concentrated flavors that are diluted and hidden by foods' natural water content.

From a culinary point of view, you can dehydrate just about anything: not only meats but also fruits, vegetables, flowers, liquids, seawater, mushrooms, roots, and grasses. Once you pull the water out, what's left behind is intense, unexpected flavor with unlimited possibilities. Take, for example, organic marigold petals. I had an idea of substituting the subtle floral aroma of edible marigold, a flower ubiquitous in Hindu culture, for the more traditional turmeric to create a beautiful new version of curry powder. It turned out to be one of the most interesting things I've ever tasted. In my restaurants, most of what we dehydrate is used as garnish (tomatoes, mushrooms, beet "chips") or ground down to a powder that dusts a plate, usually echoing the main ingredient. For instance, when we make braised beef short ribs, we'll dehydrate more of the vegetables used in the braise (carrots, onions, turnips, and herbs) to finish the dish. The intense color pop is beautiful, and the flavor makes complete sense. We use an expensive professional dehydrator, but it is by no means essential for dehydrating at home.

The process is simple. Line a baking sheet with parchment paper and oil lightly. Arrange thin slices of—you name it—evenly on the baking sheet and place it in an oven set to the lowest possible temperature: 170° to 200°F is ideal. (Anything warmer and the natural sugars in the food will caramelize or even burn.) Drying times are determined by the moisture levels of the food you are dehydrating: 45 minutes for sliced mushrooms, or as long as 6 hours for Roma tomatoes. Because most ovens have hot spots, rotating the baking sheet every few hours is a good idea for consistent drying.

THANK YOU

I would like to thank the following people, without whom this book would not have been possible:

My lovely wife, Tolan. We've written so many books together, our new anniversary is a pub date. Thanks for keeping it under control, and for being an amazing mother to our three beautiful children, Miles, Hayden, and Dorothy, as well as an incredible business partner. I love you with all of my heart.

Pam Krauss, my mentor and trusted editor, six books deep. We met in 2000 on set at Food Network, she published my first book a year later, and has been one of the dearest, most invested friends I've ever had the privilege of knowing. I think this is our best work . . . for now.

John Lee, my photographer. Thanks for bringing such a high level of creativity to our projects. This is our fourth book together and you keep blowing me away. I've found my cookbook soul mate. I love your pictures. Thanks to Jen and Theo for giving up so much of your time.

Anthony Hoy Fong. Just shy of a decade, you and I together have ridden this crazy roller coaster called life through eight seasons of *Tyler's Ultimate,* five cookbooks, and travels, doing demos in fifty-plus cities some years. Your business mind and attention to detail are incredible, not to mention you're one hell of a good cook. Thanks for cowriting the recipes with me. They're beautifully expressed and tested down to a grain of salt. And from you, I would expect nothing less than perfection. Our love to Kai.

The Florence Group team: Adam Block, Donna Perreault, John Mucci, Diane Melkonian, Richard Eisenberg, Lisa Shotland, and Michael Psaltis. You guys fight the good fight every day and I love and respect you all for what you do for us.

A deep and special thank-you to my team, business partners and associates, who share the dream, sacrifice, drive, determination, and love for all things delicious:

The dedicated team at our Kitchen Shop. We just celebrated our fourth anniversary and the shop has never looked better. I'm super proud of what we are doing there. Thank you, Tamara Kennedy, Kathe Murray, Jessica Blanco, Billy McCubbin, Ashley Sanchez, and the entire staff.

Mike and Kristen House, Rick Ronald and Anne Harper, Tony and Michele Marcell, John Gurnee, Will Hughins, Matt Masera, Kyle McKibbin, Ken Wagstaff, Adam Betts, Joel Rivas, Brian Terra, and the entire staff of Wayfare Tavern. I can't believe our little restaurant is two years old. Thanks for your friendship, dedication, and passion and for making Wayfare Tavern amazing. Here's to many, many more years serving San Francisco, the greatest city in the world.

Sammy and Kari Hagar, our sensational operations director David Sturno, Remy Wilson, Preston Clark, Phil Prigoff, and the entire staff of El Paseo in Mill Valley. Breathing life back into the old bones of one of the most beautiful restaurants in the country has been truly special. I'm proud to work with you all and thank you for making El Paseo such a hit. Preston, good luck back in New York; I'll miss you, my friend.

My Sprout family: cofounders Max and Jillian MacKenzie, Dan Heiges, Richard Harford, Geoff Stella, Jonathan Old, Walter Freedman, Dennis Hersch, David McKane, and especially our tireless CEO, Ron Davis. Thank you for all your hard work. We all stand for such integrity, making the best, most nutritional organic baby food that we can. We hope to help create the first new healthy generation in America in the last fifty years.

The Michael Mondavi family: Rob Jr. and Lydia, Michael, Isabel, and Dina. Ten medals in two seasons—I think we're onto something. Making wine together has truly been a highlight of my career. Thank you, Tony Coltrin; you have an incredible palate and it's a pleasure blending wine with you. And Irene Habermeier for your tireless patience and attention to detail.

My Food Network family. Sixteen years and going strong; it's never been a more fulfilling experience. Thank you for everything, Brooke Johnson, Bob Tuschman, Brian Lando, and Allison Page, as well as Dean Ollins and Tom Forman from Relativity Real for three incredible seasons of *The Great Food Truck Race.*

To my amazing airport team at SFO, Taste on the Fly: Adam Light, Michael Levine, Richard Hoff, and Patty Blecha. I love what we're doing at Tyler Florence Fresh—a first-class picnic at the airport, flying at cruising altitude.

Our special events partner, Laurie Arons, and everyone at Paula LeDuc Catering.

To our friends and family who are there for us every day: Marge and Larry, Jordan and Jenny, Kuncle Cavan, Janet and Chuck, Lala, Alana, Bill and Vanessa, Nina and Chris, Shara and Scott, Michael and Michael, Greg and Gary, Anna and James, the Guncles, and the entire DeBartolo family.

Last but not least, **Crown and Clarkson Potter/Publishers,** especially Jane Treuhaft, Christine Tanigawa, and designer Jan Derevjanik. A huge thank-you not only for publishing my book but for being the beacon of rectitude in food literature.

INDEX